Cognitive-Behavioral Therapy of Schizophrenia

David G. Kingdon

and

Douglas Turkington
Bassetlaw Hospital
Nottinghamshire, UK

Foreword by Aaron T. Beck

PSYCHOLOGY PRESS
ALERE FLAMMAM
· Taylor & Francis Group ·

Reprinted 1995 and 2000

Published in the United Kingdom by
Psychology Press
27 Church Road
Hove
East Sussex
BN3 2FA

Published in the United States by the The Guilford Press

British Library Cataloguing in Publication Data
A catalogue record for this book is available from the British Library

ISBN 0–86377–328–1 (hbk)
ISBN 0–86377–329–X (pbk)

Printed and bound in the UK by Biddles Ltd, Guildford and King's Lynn

Cognitive–Behavioral
Therapy of Schizophrenia

It is a pleasure to write the foreword to this impressive volume by Kingdon and Turkington, and to give it my personal endorsement. One of the great merits of their book is the distinction it makes between the diagnosis of "schizophrenia" and the label of "insanity." The fact that patients diagnosed as "schizophrenic" have a circumscribed set of irrational beliefs does not mean that they are irrational individuals. How discouraging it must be to patients with specific delusions or hallucinations to have to face the stigma of being pigeonholed as "mentally ill," or even at times "crazy" or "insane." The continuous watchfulness, apprehension, and mutual misunderstandings of their families and friends, compounded by subtle and sometimes outright rejection by society as a whole, aggravate the profound personal difficulties presented by the illness itself.

When persons with schizophrenia begin to consider themselves as outcasts of society and irrevocably ill, it is not surprising that a large number of them become depressed, demoralized, and hopeless. Depressed schizophrenic patients have the highest suicide rate of any patient group. Thus, this book is of value in providing a promising approach—and a new challenge—to the problems of patients with this disorder.

I have found Kingdon and Turkingtons's book delightful to read and eminently sensible. Their model of schizophrenia has a good deal in common with the cognitive model of panic disorder, which has proved highly useful. Like the work on panic disorder, this work on schizophrenia presents a novel conceptualization that provides an alternate meaning for symptoms, lends itself to intervention, can be supported by a variety of data and observations, and is easily explained and taught.

Aside from destigmatizing the diagnosis of schizophrenia and offering a new approach for those disabled by this condition, the book is a treasure in that it shows that these patients can learn to use an asset within themselves—their own rationality—to combat the ravages of their illness. Kingdon and Turkington have performed a great service by offering a treatment that expands the options for people who have a schizophrenic disorder. Thus, the patients can progress beyond simply taking drugs and participating in the various activities provided in the hospital or in the aftercare units: *They can become active agents in their own recovery.* They no longer have to be content with simply being passive recipients of medication and other forms of treatment, but can actively apply the strategies and techniques of cognitive therapy.

Since cognitive therapy is a learning process, I believe that the patients who receive this form of treatment—in addition to standard treatment of schizophrenia—will be able to deal more effectively with the usual stressors of life and will be much less subject to relapse. I expect that the patients will show more progress when cognitive therapy is combined with drug treatment; in fact, they may be able to reduce the dosage of drugs, and in some cases to eliminate them completely.

My review of the cases described by Kingdon and Turkington has persuaded me that they have opened up a whole new vista in the treatment of schizophrenia. Of course, controlled studies and long-term follow-up will be necessary to establish the precise position of this new approach in the treatment of schizophrenia. However, this approach is available to be adapted by mental health workers already trained in psychotherapy, particularly those with a background in cognitive–behavioral therapy. This treatment should prove to be helpful in the same way that the cognitive therapy of other disorders has proven to be effective.

This book will give a "shot in the arm" to clinicians interested in working with psychotic patients. The idea that delusions merely occupy one endpoint on a continuum of degrees of belief, which the authors develop with finesse, will certainly help clinicians to feel justified in using cognitive techniques with such patients. Similarly, other observations and findings on schizophrenia (e.g., the observation that only a minority of patients are on a deteriorating course) will aid the morale of therapists as well as that of patients. The observations of this volume are certainly consistent with my limited experience with psychotic patients.

This publication indeed has a personal meaning to me. When I first started using and talking about cognitive therapy in the early 1960s, I thought that this therapy would be largely limited to patients with various neuroses, such as depression, anxiety disorder, phobias, and the like. When professionals at seminars and conferences asked me to state conditions for which cognitive therapy was not indicated, I would say, "Schizophrenia." It is a pleasant surprise now to see that I was wrong—cognitive therapy does have a direct application to this disorder.

It is of some interest that the present authors have reminded me that 40 years ago, in 1952, I published a paper on the psychotherapy of a case of chronic schizophrenia with delusions. In that paper, I described how I utilized a variety of methods, including several strategies that have been expanded and refined by Kingdon and Turkington. First, I gave the patient a plausible or "normal" explanation for his delusions; second, I induced the patient to apply systematic reality testing to various aspects of his delusion. To my surprise, his delusions gradually disappeared. Later, I collaborated on a study with Richard Hole and John Rush (Hole, Rush, & Beck, 1979) in which cognitive interventions were applied in a more systematic way with the delusions of several patients who had schizophrenia. Again, the results were very promising.

Considerable time elapsed before this approach was expanded and incorporated into a broad therapeutic program and used in a systematic way in a large group of patients. For this, I am enormously grateful to the present authors, and I believe that readers will be grateful likewise. It is my expectation that the present volume will make this approach available to a vast army of mental health workers who are struggling with the difficult problems of this disorder, and, at the same time, will provide new hope for patients with schizophrenia.

Aaron T. Beck
University of Pennsylvania

ACKNOWLEDGMENTS

We wish to acknowledge the many colleagues—including Patrick Loftus; Paul Gilbert; Norman MacAskill; John Reed; Paul Bebbington; Liz Kuipers; Tom Sensky; Jan Scott and others at the Newcastle Cognitive Therapy Centre; Professor Alec Jenner; Professor John Strauss; and Professor Carlo Perris—who provided encouragement and with whom these ideas have been discussed over the past few years. We are indebted to Dr. Aaron T. Beck for developing the techniques on which this work is based and for nurturing cognitive therapists worldwide. We are especially grateful to him for writing the foreword to this book. Finally, without the patients and staff members of Bassetlaw Health Authority—especially our secretary, Diane Nelson—these ideas could not have been put into practice.

A preliminary report of this work has been published in the *Journal of Nervous and Mental Disease* (Kingdon & Turkington, 1991a); a review has appeared in *Social Psychiatry and Psychiatric Epidemilogy* (Kingdon & Turkington, 1991b); and a patient study has been published in the *British Journal of Psychiatry* (Turkington & Kingdon, 1991).

C O N T E N T S

Reasoning-based approaches have been used since time immemorial in attempts to change people's unusual beliefs and attitudes. The Stoics believed that people upset themselves because of the beliefs they held about the events occurring in their lives. As such, it was not only possible but in part the responsibility of each individual to change these interpretations (Hadas, 1962).

Such ideas were put into a therapeutic format for the treatment of neuroses by Beck (Beck et al., 1979, 1985). Anxiety-provoking beliefs working through faulty general interpretations (e.g., overgeneralization from one event to other unrelated events), and eventually through automatic thoughts (e.g., "I'm going to die; I can't cope"), were shown to be amenable to cognitive therapy. The same mechanisms have been shown to operate in depression, anger, jealousy, and other states of emotional distress. However, reasoning-based approaches to schizophrenia in the past have tended to be relatively confrontational in style and have met with little success. Is it possible that a more structured reasoning-based approach might be more successful?

A central feature of schizophrenia is a disruption of thought processes, such that illogical associations are made between events that most of us would not believe to be connected. It can usually be diagnosed in late adolescence from the development of strange behavior (e.g., withdrawal, frightened responses to paranoid beliefs, and the holding of strange postures) and delusions (seemingly irrational beliefs). The individual may also hear voices that, although seeming to come from outside themselves, originate within.

Over the past 20 years, diagnosis of schizophrenia has

become increasingly reliable with the development of the Research Diagnostic Criteria (Spitzer et al., 1975), on which the criteria in the *Diagnostic and Statistical Manuals* of the American Psychiatric Association and the *International Classification of Diseases* of the World Health Organization have been based (see Tables Int.1 and Int.2). Schizophrenia directly affects almost 1 in every 100 of the population at some point in life. It presents a colossal burden to caregivers and the community in general in terms of distress and disability. In addition, the fear of "madness" itself is probably ubiquitous to a lesser or greater extent.

Medication has proved of considerable benefit in reducing the severity of symptoms of schizophrenia, at times eradicating them, and reducing their recurrence. But there remain many patients with significant disabilities in whom medication is ineffective (at least partially). Even drugs such as clozapine for resistant symptoms only appear effective in up to a third of those for whom they are indicated; side effects further limit the use of medication. Other patients cannot be persuaded to take it because of the very nature of the illness itself. They do not see why they should take medication, because as they see it, they do not have a "medical" problem. Poor or erratic compliance is a major problem affecting up to 75% in first-episode schizophrenia (Kissling, 1992), and up to 50% of patients discharged from a hospital in one study failed to take even 75% of the medication prescribed (Buchanan, 1992).

Psychotherapy techniques based on psychoanalysis have not proved beneficial in treatment of this group, but the development of cognitive–behavioral therapy, which is more focused and structured, does hold promise for the future. The particular techniques discussed in this book are directed specifically at the thinking patterns that patients have or develop—hence *cognitive* therapy. The aim is by reasoning processes to modify these apparently fixed beliefs, faulty interpretations, and automatic thoughts, and by relating them to "normal experience" to reduce some of the fear attached to them.

It was while working on the Nottingham Neurosis Study (Tyrer et al., 1988, 1990), in which cognitive therapy was

TABLE Int.1. Criteria for Schizophrenia: *International Classification of Diseases,* **10th Revision (ICD-10)**

At least one of the following:
    abnormal subjective experiences, such as:
        thought echo, insertion, withdrawal, broadcasting
        the will being replaced by some alien agency so that actions, speech, or
            feeling no longer seem to be under the control of the self
        delusional perceptions—something seen or heard becomes immediately
            invested with a special meaning
    delusion of control, influence, or passivity
    bizarre delusions of other kinds
    auditory hallucinations in clear conciousness, taking the form:
        of commentary on thoughts and actions
        of voices discussing the person between themselves
        of voices coming from some part of the body

Or at least two of the following:
    delusions of any content if accompanied by hallucinations in any
        modality
    hallucinatory voices of any kind
      which occur for every day for weeks
      or most days for months on end
    marked thought and speech disorder
      with prominent incoherence, irrelevance, sudden interruptions
      neologisms and incomprehensibility
    catatonic disturbances
      excitement, stupor, mutism
      negativism, posturing, waxy flexibility
    marked social withdrawal and lowering of social performance,
        accompanied by blunted or inappropriate affect

For *at least one month*

Criteria for schizophrenia present *before* criteria for mood disturbance met if
        patient meets criteria for manic or depressive episode

Disorder *not* attributable to:
    organic brain disease
    alcohol dependence
    drug intoxication or withdrawal

Note. Adapted from World Health Organization (1992). Copyright 1992 by the World Health Organization. Adapted by permission.

TABLE Int.2. Criteria for Schizophrenia: *Diagnostic and Statistical Manual of Mental Disorders*, **Fourth Edition (DSM-IV Draft)**

A. Characteristic Symptoms: At least two of the following, each present for a significant portion of time during a one month period (or less if successfully treated):

   (1) delusions
   (2) hallucinations
   (3) disorganized speech (e.g., frequent derailment or incoherence)
   (4) grossly disorganized or catatonic behavior
   (5) negative symptoms, i.e., affective flattening, alogia, or avolition

   [Note: Only one A symptom is required if delusions are bizarre or hallucinations consist of a voice keeping up a running commentary on the person's behavior or thoughts, or two or more voices conversing with each other.]

B. Social/Occupational Dysfunction: For a significant portion of the time since the onset of the disturbance, one or more major areas of functioning such as work, interpersonal relations or self-care is markedly below the level achieved prior to the onset (or when the onset is in childhood or adolescence, failure to achieve expected level of interpersonal, academic, or occupational achievement).

C. Duration: Continuous signs of the disturbance persist for at least six months. This six-month period must include at least one month of symptoms that meet criterion A (i.e., active phase symptoms), and may include periods of prodromal or residual symptoms. During these prodromal or residual periods, the signs of the disturbance may be manifested by only negative symptoms or two or more symptoms listed in criterion A present in an attenuated form (e.g., odd beliefs, unusual perceptual experiences).

D. Schizoaffective and Mood Disorder Exclusion: Schizoaffective Disorder and Mood Disorder with Psychotic Features have been ruled out because either: (1) no major depressive or manic episodes have occurred concurrently with the active phase symptoms; or (2) if mood episodes have occurred during active phase symptoms, their total duration has been brief relative to the duration of the active and residual periods.

E. Substance/General Medical Condition Exclusion: The disturbance is not due to the direct effects of a substance (e.g., drugs of abuse, medication) or a general medical condition.

Note. Adapted from American Psychiatric Association (1993). Copyright 1993 by the American Psychiatric Association. Adapted by permission.

employed with a group of patients with neurotic disorders, that it became apparent to one of us (Kingdon) that the techniques he was using with patients who had psychoses could be described as a variant of cognitive therapy. We have gradually defined the techniques used, incorporated additional components, and refined them with further study of the literature. The ideas were conceived over a 15-year period and have been consolidated over the past 4. There remains much scope for their further development.

In our unselected group of patients, women were considerably outnumbered by men; the male–female ratio was more than 2:1. We have therefore, to save repetition, used masculine pronouns to refer to a patient in general terms. The term "patient" is used to indicate a person who has developed signs and symptoms of schizophrenia to such an extent that he is deemed in need of treatment and entitled to certain benefits of the "sick role." This means that he becomes eligible under the British social security system for "sickness certification"— that is, he is excused from working or seeking a job during this period—and is generally considered, to a variable degree, entitled to support of a practical and emotional nature. The expectations that others have of him in response is that he will accept medical assistance subject to his level of insight into his situation, and will essentially do what he can to recover to his previous level of health where this is possible (Mayou, 1984). Not all people with schizophrenia are therefore necessarily patients at any one time. Some may be able to function without this social support, despite continuing to have symptoms of the illness. Clearly, those who have recovered from its effects (including those related to their drive and motivation) should no longer be considered patients; the fact that so frequently others assume "once a schizophrenic, always a schizophrenic" is one of the problems this book aims to address.

We begin with a discussion of the theoretical background to the "normalizing" rationale and the cognitive–behavioral techniques; this includes a discussion of relevant research into cognitive approaches. As in all cognitive therapies, behavioral strategies are used at certain points in treatment. This part of the book is followed by a "treatment manual" that was initially developed for use in workshop settings and as a basis for structured evaluation. Patient studies are interspersed throughout this section to provide illustrative material. Speculations about evaluation and evolution of the techniques conclude the book. You may wish to start at the beginning and finish at the end. Alternatively, you can dive into the patient studies first and then browse through the theoretical background, or simply get "stuck into" the treatment section. Whichever course you may wish to take, we hope the book interests, informs, and most importantly inspires you to look a little closer for what can be understood in your patient's, your relative's, or even your own schizophrenia.

THEORETICAL
BACKGROUND

Explanations of Schizophrenia

Knowledge, understanding, and fear are bound together, so that the fear of the unknown is perhaps the greatest fear of all. If people know what they are faced with, they can devise a strategy to cope with or even overcome it. And even if they are faced with an overwhelming situation, they can at least adjust psychologically to the consequences they can see developing. Not knowing, just fearing, is commonly the situation both with those suffering from schizophrenia and with those caring for and about them. Providing a framework, however tentative, on which they can base an understanding of the confusing and frightening experiences of schizophrenia would seem likely to provide reassurance, reduce anxiety, and ease feelings of depression;, in other words, it may have direct therapeutic potential. In an investigation of coping strategies described in more detail later, Carr (1988) goes still further and suggests "the admittedly speculative notion that the timely introduction of a plausible objective explanation for subjectively inexplicable experience could perhaps inhibit the development of delusional beliefs, the basic characteristic of madness" (p. 341).

In the treatment of depression (Beck et al., 1979) or anxiety (Beck et al., 1985), providing an explanation of the symptoms involved is fundamental to the application of cognitive therapy. Similarly, explanations of schizophrenic symptoms would seem to be necessary if we are to develop the use of cognitive therapies in treating schizophrenia. Such explanations may be biological, psychological, or social. Alternatively, they may be multifaceted, with elements of all three. Biological theories are based on genetic, neuropathological, and neurochemical findings (reviewed by Murray et al., 1988); psychological theories are based on psychoanalytic theory (e.g., Arieti, 1979); and social theories are based on theories of stigmatization (Goffman, 1961) and labeling (Scheff, 1963), perceived abnormal family dynamics (Bateson et al., 1956), and societal pressures (Laing, 1960).

Laing and Esterson (1964) specifically aimed to demonstrate the "social intelligibility" of what "psychiatrists . . . call . . . schizophrenia" (p. 11)—that is, to produce explanations demonstrating how schizophrenia can be understood in a social, particularly a family, context. However, their work has been interpreted as "blaming" the family and society in general for schizophrenia (Hudson, 1975), which has been a factor in its rejection by most psychiatrists. Unfortunately, but understandably, some families have taken this work to mean that they are responsible in some way for their relatives' illness. Not surprisingly, there have been difficulties in validating the conclusions reached in comparative studies with nonschizophrenic families.

Laing's publications are widely available and thus have been read by those both in and outside the mental health professions; their influence on social and political changes, particularly the move toward "normalization" philosophies and specifically "care in the community," has quite probably been more profound than is currently recognized. Nevertheless, their incorporation into individual management of the patient group that it has such difficulty defining has probably been limited.

PATIENT'S OWN EXPLANATIONS

It is important to recognize that patients develop their own explanations of what is happening to them, and these can be extremely varied. Romme, a Dutch psychiatrist, and colleagues (Romme & Escher, 1989; Romme et al., 1992) describe the importance to their group of patient who all heard "voices" of developing rationales for their symptoms as a method of coping with them. Their interest in this began when one of Romme's patients described reading *The Origin of Consciousness in the Breakdown of the Bicameral Mind* by Jaynes (1976). She found helpful his statement that "hearing voices [was] the normal way of making decisions until about 1300 b.c.," and that "hearing voices has disappeared and been replaced by what we now call 'consciousness'" (Romme, 1989, p. 207). After this patient and Romme appreared on a television program to describe this, 450 people who heard voices made contact with them.

A great many frames of reference were used by this group—psychodynamic, mystical, parapsychological, and medical. Jung's work appealed to many, with his suggestion that "impulses from the unconscious speak to humans in visions or voices" (Romme, 1989, p. 213). Some felt that reading his books helped them to develop a better understanding of their voices. Others subscribed to the psychodynamic theory that trauma repressed returns to consciousness in the form of flashbacks, "feeling pursued," aggressive voices, or terrifying images. Mystics, it was said by some, "often assume they know that people have the capacity to expand their consciousness by developing spirituality. Voices may be viewed as part of that expansion" (Romme, 1989, p. 213). In parapsychology, "voices may be viewed as originating from a special gift or sensitivity" (p. 213). Biological or medical explanations were based on our current understanding of how the use of medication alleviates symptoms through receptor blockade. Romme and colleagues cautioned, however, that explanations placing the phenomena beyond the patients' grasp or influence could be unhelpful to them in coping, and in fact could induce feelings of hopelessness. Thus it seems that providing a purely medical explanation of schizophrenia may lead to alienation, depression, and poor compliance with treatment.

Increasing amounts of psychoeducational material about

schizophrenia have been produced over the last decade. However, as Ascher-Svanum (1989) has commented, most psychoeducational programs have been designed for family members rather than patients themselves. This is clearly evident from a survey of the otherwise excellent pamphlets (e.g., Leff et al., 1987) and books (e.g., Arieti, 1979; Kuipers & Bebbington, 1987) readily available in the United Kingdom, which are virtually all written for the caregiver or professional. Ascher-Svanum (1989), however, describes a program aimed at increasing compliance with medical treatment, which uses both didactic and experiential techniques to educate patients. She discusses with patients the nature of schizophrenia, causes, prevalence, drug treatments, and the use of community resources (including advocacy). Such programs may be becoming increasingly common, but nevertheless the relative neglect of educating the patient about his own illness needs to be noted.

This neglect also needs to be questioned. It may be occurring because untested assumptions are made that patients will be unable to participate in educational programs. When a patient is catatonic or grossly thought-disordered, this may be the case, but in most circumstances this seems to be patently untrue. Such assumptions probably demonstrate the extent of "catastrophization" among mental health professionals in relation to schizophrenia. Overgeneralization from a stereotype also seems to be occurring. It is likely that even the most disabled patients are far more aware of surrounding events and circumstances than may be apparent, and that even if participation is initially minimal, explanations as part of a rehabilitation program can be therapeutic. Failing to give even inadequate explanations and to involve a patient in his own treatment program—perhaps just giving such information to relatives, or not at all—must increase the patient's paranoia, helplessness, and even belief that control of his own life is not in his hands. This may even exacerbate or precipitate delusions that the patient is being controlled by external forces or simply other people (i.e., "passivity phenomena"). As such, current practice could be a factor contributing toward failure to recover.

DISTINCTIONS BETWEEN SCHIZOPHRENIC AND "NORMAL" EXPERIENCE?

Current psychiatric practice emphasizes distinctions between schizophrenic symptoms and "normal" experience, ostensibly to simplify diagnosis and classification. This can, however, make understanding of the symptoms more difficult than if they could be related to culturally or personally familiar experiences. Such distinctions also more readily lead to stigmatization of a patient by others, lowering his self-esteem. Finally, such divisions would seem to be quite artificial.

Strauss (1969) examined Present State Examination data collected as part of the World Health Organization's (1973) International Pilot Study of Schizophrenia. A total of 119 patients were interviewed. The researchers found that many of the responses to their questions were difficult to categorize precisely. They scored half as many delusions "questionable" as they did "definite," and three-quarters as many hallucinations "questionable" as "definite." Their difficulties arose from consideration of "external reality factors" (e.g., fundamentalist religious training) and uncertainties about, for example, voices heard through walls, which might be misinterpretations of things said rather than true hallucinations. Some of this uncertainty could presumably have been resolved if an interviewer had been in possession of more relevant information— if, for example, the interviewer had been with the patient when he heard voices through the wall and could determine whether misinterpretation was occurring.

Nevertheless, on the basis of the evidence as a whole, Strauss (1969) concluded that "phenomena like delusions and hallucinations represent points on continua function" (p. 586). In a later paper (Strauss, 1989), he expanded this to say that "all intermediate gradations of experience exist, from normal perception to hallucinations and from normal ideation to delusions. . . . many patients, for example, experience something that is more perceptual than just a strange idea but is not quite a voice" (p. 27). This is not a new assertion; Sedman (1966b) reported that in 1911, "Jaspers . . . pointed out [that] there is an infinite variety of image-phenomena ranging from normal imagery to fully developed pseudo-hallucinations" (p. 489). This view was substantiated later in a comparative study of imagery and pseudohallucinations (Sedman, 1966a).

Strauss (1989) also stressed the importance of following patients over time, as considerable evidence indicates that "over periods of improvement symptoms may fade slowly through intermediate levels of experience. Hallucinations may be more and more dimly perceived until they disappear entirely. Delusions can gradually lose their power and then cease to exist" (p. 27). Strauss (1969) did not suggest, as others have done, that schizophrenia does not exist, but that "schizophrenia . . . might be more adequately described as a point or a series of points on a functional continuum" (p. 585). He added that

> schizophrenia and the symptoms that characterise it are understandable exaggerations of normal function and not exotic symptoms superimposed on the personality. When the distortions and exaggeration of certain psychological functions reach a certain level of eccentricity or begin to impair social function they are called symptoms. (p. 585)

Strauss (1969) suggested that "tentative criteria for defining the continua" (and thus where normal behavior merges into that of schizophrenia) are as follows:

1. The degree of the patient's conviction of the objective reality of the bizarre experience (how strongly he holds it).
2. The degree of absence of direct cultural or stimulus determination of an experience (how unrelated it appears to be to his situation).
3. Amount of time spent preoccupied with the experience.
4. Implausibility of the experience (e.g., seeing a man from Mars, as compared to mistaking seeing a car outside one's house [and thinking it related to himself, how unlikely the experience appears to be]). (p. 586)

Psychopathological terminology (i.e., the language of the

science of mental disorders) also provides some evidence for functional continua—for example, in the use of the term "pseudohallucination." This term has been used in two alternative intermediate ways (Kraupl-Taylor, 1981) as referring to "self-recognized hallucinations" or to "introspected images of great vividness and spontaneity" (p. 265).

The use of "overvalued ideas" as a term referring to beliefs which are neither normal or delusional, but somewhere in between, also suggests at least gradations of experience. McKenna (1984) reported that Wernicke established the concept as

> a solitary belief that came to determine an individual's actions to a morbid degree, while at the same time justified and a normal expression of his nature . . . [which] could sometimes progress to full psychosis. . . . [Over-valued ideas] . . . grew out of adverse experience in a way which made it comprehensible. (p. 579)

McKenna has suggested that

> passionate political, religious and ethical convictions are as inextricably bound up with personality and experience, arise just as unpredictably, and have the same ability to alter an individual's whole way of life. The overvalued idea may thus be only the pathological expression of a pattern of behavior of which we are all capable. (p. 584)

In developing an acceptable explanation of schizophrenia, the work discussed here is fundamentally important, because the danger with categorical definitions (e.g., biological explanations as presented currently) in relation to dimensional ones is that the former require a change in type rather than degree. They can be stigmatizing, in that they imply that a patient is different in some distinct way from others, rather than being the same "only more so." It is less threatening to other people—perhaps to their own sanity—to think of someone acting in a bizarre or embarrassing way as a different sort of person or somebody clearly distinct in some way.

However, it would be wrong to think that schizophrenia is any less serious a disorder because its symptoms may be on a continuum with normal experience. A medical analogy may be made with high blood pressure, which can cause very serious problems if untreated, but is nevertheless on a continuum with normal blood pressure.

"SCHIZOPHRENIC" SYMPTOMS IN "NORMAL" EXPERIENCE

Having considered evidence that symptoms of schizophrenia can blend into "normality" in those diagnosed as having schizophrenia, one would anticipate the reverse to be possible, that is, that "normal" people (i.e., people who do not have schizophrenia) should demonstrate symptoms that blend into schizophrenia. And, indeed, a considerable but neglected body of research attests to the occurrence in normal subjects of symptoms and signs similar, if not always identical, to those associated with schizophrenia.

Hallucinations, delusions, and thought disorder can occur in organic confusional states—for example, severe infections, delirium tremens caused by alcohol withdrawal, and states induced by drugs (e.g., cocaine, amphetamines, and LSD)—which are well recognized as producing psychopathological phenomena indistinguishable from those in schizophrenia. They can cause diagnostic confusion because of this; they take precedence over schizophrenia in the most commonly used classification systems, the World Health Organization's (1992) *International Classification of Diseases* (10th revision), and the American Psychiatric Association's (1993) *Diagnostic and Statistical Manual of Mental Disorders* (fourth edition, draft). In other words, in the presence of a clear physical cause for psychological symptoms, a diagnosis of schizophrenia is not made. This is presumably because the underlying disorder generally is what is treated (although some symptomatic treatment may be temporarily necessary), and the longer-term prognosis is determined by the physical problem rather than being that of schizophrenia. Drug-induced psychoses are of particular interest in this context.

Fischman (1983) has reviewed the relationship between drug-induced psychoses, particularly where LSD has been involved, and schizophrenia. In the 1950s and early 1960s many psychiatrists used the drug (under suitably controlled conditions) to attempt to gain insight into how someone with schizophrenia feels and thinks. Early work did suggest considerable similarities, although some researchers have since described significant differences. This later work has been criticized in turn for its use of patients with chronic schizophrenia for comparative purposes, rather than those with acute illnesses. Fischman describes as common to drug states and acute psychosis an "experience of heightened awareness" and an awareness of "significance," the experience of expanded relevance or meaning described by Jaspers (1913/1963) as the initial stage in the development of delusional thinking. Fischman's conclusion is that certain fundamental areas of convergence between drug and schizophrenic states can be demonstrated. Not infrequently, patients who later develop schizophrenia have been through periods of such drug abuse, but it is unclear whether this has had any causative role. Our experience has been that some of the most disabled in our group of patients have had such experiences, but it is possible that a common denominator can be found in personality traits predisposing to drug use and severity of illness.

Schizophrenic symptoms and signs have also been shown to occur in situations that have no clear organic basis. Examples include hostage situations (Siegel, 1984); solitary confinement (Grassian, 1983); and conditions of food and water deprivation, as well as sleep deprivation (Oswald, 1974) and sensory deprivation (Vernon, 1963). The last two forms of deprivation are discussed here in some detail.

Knowledge of the effects of sensory deprivation goes back to the ancient Greeks (Slade, 1984). However, the original pioneering experiments were performed by Hebb and colleagues at McGill University (Bexton et al., 1954). Their original descriptions involved deprivation periods using confinement of up to 2–3 days, after which they noted that it was difficult to persuade volunteers to stay. This compares with much shorter periods in later experiments (e.g., Leff, 1968). Bexton et. al. (1954) commented that

> among our early subjects there were several references, rather puzzling at first, to what one of them described as "dreaming awake." Then one of us, while serving as a subject, observed the phenomenon [that is, hallucinatory experiences] and realized its peculiarity and extent. (p. 73)

Different levels of complexity of these phenomena were noted. Between 1961 and 1965, considerable interest in sensory deprivation was generated; Slade (1984) found 322 articles published in that time and 483 in all. The alternative types of perceptual deprivation developed were as follows:

1. Deprivation without bodily confinement, in which patients remained alone on a bed in a sound- and light-proofed room, but were able to move about and in most experiments to leave the room briefly in order to use the toilet.
2. Deprivation with bodily confinement—for example, by suspension in a water tank.

Very few volunteers have tolerated more than 10 hours of water tank confinement, whereas many have completed more than 7 days of bed confinement. The former appears to produce greater deleterious effects than the latter, as one might anticipate.

Slade (1984) noted that "the original reports of the McGill University studies indicated severe mental symptoms in virtually all subjects, including both visual and auditory hallucinations" (p. 258). However, the early workers used a rather loose definition of hallucination, and attempts were made to employ more precise descriptive terms. The concepts of "reported visual sensations" and "reported auditory sensations" were developed. Each category was subdivided into "Type A" (meaningless sensations) and "Type B" (meaningful, integrated sensations). Overall, 50% of subjects experienced Type A sensations of both types, 20% experienced Type B visual sensations, and 15% experienced Type B auditory sensations in experimental situations of sensory deprivation reported (Slade, 1984).

There therefore appears to be a continuum of sensation reaching up to clearly formed hallucinations in a few vulnerable individuals. Ethical limitations necessarily preclude the continuation of such experiments for indefinite periods but it seems likely that more people, perhaps a majority, might hallucinate if stressed sufficiently. It is also noteworthy that participants volunteered for these experiments; we know nothing about those who would not have been prepared to take part. Volunteers were also clearly aware of the safety precautions and were being checked regularly.

However, involuntary confinement does occur (although certainly not in controlled research environments), in hostage situations. In these circumstances, hallucinations have also been found to occur in many subjects (Siegel, 1984).

A further finding in sensory deprivation of significance is that of increased suggestibility. An early study at McGill University (Scott, quoted in Slade, 1984) presented students with a one-sided account of psychic phenomena that was designed to persuade them of the existence of such forces. One group was subjected at the same time to conditions of sensory deprivation, whereas the other was not; the experimental sensory deprived group showed greater attitude change (i.e., the subjects became more accepting of the existence of psychic phenomena) than the control group. (See Chapter 4 for further discussion of this topic.)

Leff (1968) repeated the original sensory deprivation work under controlled conditions, but apparently at lower levels of deprivation. His subjects described "vivid fleeting visual images . . . very like the images of dreams" (p. 1504). He found a highly significant association between "schizoid personality and the reporting of perceptual experiences" (p. 1506) and noted that "the significance of this finding rests on the assumption that there is a close link between schizoid personality traits and schizophrenia" (p. 1506). Leff reviewed

evidence, confirmed by his study, that subjects with higher
anxiety levels tolerated sensory deprivation less well, and
found a significant association with the reporting of perceptual experiences. Thus the more anxious the subjects were, the
more likely they were to hallucinate. His conclusion was that
"this investigation has shown that the perceptual experiences
of normal people under conditions of sensory deprivation
overlap considerably with those of mentally ill patients" (p.
1507).

Sleep deprivation appears to have been less intensively
researched. However, Oswald (1974) described experimental
work with six medical students who were kept awake for 108
hours. His descriptions of these experiments are illuminating:

> At times they made senseless remarks ... shortly after
> suddenly saying, "who to begin" one bent down and
> kissed the EEG paper. ... [A typical] sleep deprived man
> ... often describes "seeing things" ... surfaces of objects
> seem to swirl and change, the wallpaper seems to come to
> life, people or faces appear suddenly, only to vanish upon
> drawing nearer. ... "Hearing things" too is quite com-
> mon. ... [Especially] striking is the unpleasant nightmare-
> like day-dream life into which some fall ... oblique re-
> marks and veiled hints begin to be made, to indicate that
> a new understanding has dawned of how some organisa-
> tion, or the experimenters, are engaged upon some secret
> and harmful plot. (pp. 56–57)

Oswald concluded that "the irrational thinking of sleep-de-
prived persons ... resembles that of certain mental illnesses,
notably paranoid schizophrenia" (p. 59). He also mentioned
the use of sleep deprivation in producing suggestibility in
"brainwashing."

The similarity between dreams and madness has been
noted frequently throughout recorded history, ever since phe-
nomenological observations to this effect were made by Aris-
totle and Plato (these authors and those following are cited by
Fischman, 1983, p. 73). Kant stated that "the lunatic is
the wakeful dreamer." Schopenhauer wrote that "a dream is
a short-lasting psychosis, and a psychosis is a long-lasting

dream." Freud observed that "in dreams and in schizophrenia words undergo condensation and displacement . . . this produces neologisms and other transformations which characterise schizophrenic speech." He later simply remarked, "A dream, then, is a psychosis."

Fischman (1983) has concluded that there are considerable similarities between schizophrenia and dreams; as mentioned previously, experimental volunteers and occasionally patients have alluded to such similarities. A state of sleep deprivation and/or isolation is common prior to acute psychotic breakdown and ratings of psychosis and insomnia correlate strongly (Meltzer et al., 1970). Although it might be concluded that this is simply the nature of psychosis (that the more severe it is, the more disturbed sleep will be), the reverse may be as important (that the more sleep-disturbed the patient is, the more psychotic he will be). The sleep disturbance may be exacerbating, and perhaps may even have a causative role in producing, the psychotic symptoms. Brief psychotic episodes following a period of insomnia induced by overwork, caring for ill relatives, or the like often appear to take this form; they remit rapidly with adequate sleep and sedation. Relating such states to patients may have potential in explaining and destigmatizing their illness—and, as we note later, may assist in producing compliance with hospital admission (when necessary) and with medication. For patients whose sleep has been erratic, we have found that suggesting to them, "Whatever else is happening, you are clearly not sleeping properly and we need to help you rest, as it seems likely that lack of sleep worsens the problems you have," can be dramatically effective in acute situations. Patients who do not in principle agree to the use of neuroleptic medication, despite full explanations about it, may accept a dose at night purely for its sedative qualities.

CONCLUSIONS

There seems to be abundant evidence that many of the signs and symptoms normally associated with schizophrenia, even some that are considered diagnostic of it, can occur in experimental volunteers. This is particularly true of sleep and sensory deprivation. It also seems that such signs and symptoms are not categorically different from normal experience but merge into it.

As Strauss (1969) suggested, a continuum seems to exist between delusions and normal thoughts, and between hallucinations and imagination. Schizophrenia represents a position or set of positions at one extreme of that continuum. The importance of these conclusions lies, first, in the ways in which they can be used therapeutically with the individual with schizophrenia, (of which more later), and second, in how they can be used with families and others to reduce stigmatization and fear by increasing understanding. They may have particular potential in mental health promotion strategies.

Cultural Context

The influence of a person's culture on the diagnosis of mental illness is well recognized particularly in cases where the psychiatrist is of a different nationality or ethnicity. Recently the difficulties of diagnosing schizophrenia in minority communities in the United Kingdom, particularly among individuals of Afro-Caribbean origin, has been a source of controversy in relationship to this. There is also a greater diversity of culture within western and other societies than often seems to be acknowledged in a mental health context. The influence of such subcultural differences on the understanding of mental illness may be fundamental but may not be readily apparent. They are not determined by a separate language or skin color; instead, the differences are more subtle involving, for example, accent, idiom, clothing, or assumptions. The influence of such less pronounced differences on psychiatric diagnosis may be significant precisely because they are so often discounted at present. This chapter examines a few of these differences that are relevant to a diagnosis of schizophrenia.

BELIEFS IN UNSCIENTIFIC PHENOMENA

Although the development of a scientific approach to psychological processes has been of fundamental importance in psychiatry, this has led to a lack of consideration of some commonly held beliefs that are of an unscientific or parapsychological nature. It is understandable that such beliefs are disregarded because of the lack of objective evidence to support them, especially with the prevailing (and perhaps at times too narrowly) analytical rationalism of the scientific community. However, a paradox remains that belief in God or at least a spiritual dimension to existence, even among scientists, is extremely common.

In their description of results of interviews by the Gallup organization of 60,000 British adults, Cox and Cowling (1989) found that the following percentages expressed belief in various unscientific phenomena:

> 68%: God
> >50%: Thought transference between two people
> >50%: The possibility of predicting that something is going to happen before it actually does
> >25%: Ghosts (the figure rose to 33% among 18 to 34-year-olds)
> 25%: Superstitions
> 25%: Reincarnation
> 23%: Horoscopes
> 21%: The devil
> 10%: "Black magic"

Bentall and Slade (1985) reported that 17% of undergraduate students said that they often heard their thoughts being spoken aloud (which is generally considered a diagnostic symptom of schizophrenia). Stevenson (1983) found that

> between 10% and 27% of the general population report having had ... a sensory perception of another person who was not physically present.... [Most such individuals] tell few people [about their experiences], or no one.... They have heard that hallucinations are symptoms of insanity, and they have no way of knowing that such experiences are not necessarily indicators of mental illness ... many of them privately believe that their experiences include some extra-sensory or paranormal communication. (p. 1609)

Eysenck (1986) is one of the few scientists who has examined such belief in any detail. He has noted that

> belief in the reality of such phenomena has been widespread since the earliest recorded times ... [and that]

before the rise of modern science, the causation of all complex physical phenomena was very poorly understood, and hence appeals to non-material agencies (ghosts, demons, angels, sorcerers and witches) took the place of causal, scientific explanation. (p. 1002)

Parapsychological phenomena of two types have been described:

1. *Cognitive*—for example, clairvoyance, telepathy, or precognition and prophecy. Here one person is believed to have acquired knowledge of facts, or of other people's thoughts, or of future events, without the use of ordinary sensory channels; hence the term "extrasensory perception" (ESP).
2. *Physical*—that is, "psychokinesis," denoting the movement of objects or people by parapsychological means. The fall of dice or the dealing of cards is thought to be influenced by "willing" them, or objects are moved (often in a violent fashion) by "poltergeists."

Most mediums claim to be controlled by someone in the spirit realm who speaks and sometimes acts through them. Although some attempts at appropriately controlled scientific research have been made in this area, the field remains an obvious one for charlatans to enter. This occurs frequently, and repugnance at the claims they make has led most researchers and clinicians to disregard spiritual or parapsychological beliefs, at least superficially. However, there can be little doubt that despite the lack of concrete evidence, many people do retain such beliefs.

Piaget (1929/1973), in his study of the development of thinking processes, describes "spontaneous magical ideas in the adult" (p. 184). He describes involuntary imitation; for example, when a person's voice has failed him, another person may speak louder as if "to lend him . . . strength" (p. 185), or a golfer may try to influence a golf ball to roll into the hole. Some people appeal to "good fortune" by their desire to ensure that the most insignificant details of a routine are not upset—for example, before a game or an examination, or in "lucky" rituals such as card players use. The relevance of such beliefs to psychotic illness has rarely been noted, but they may be of significance. As Tissot and Burnand (1980) commented in their investigation of thought disorder in schizophrenia (described in more detail later), "when rational explanations and the certainty they produce [are] lacking, magical causality and subjective certainty take their place" (p. 663).

Disorders of the possession of thought, such as thought broadcasting and insertion, have culturally accepted equivalents in beliefs in telepathy. One standardized psychiatric diagnostic instrument, the Present State Examination (Wing et al., 1974), recognizes this by inquiring of the subject, "Is anything like hypnotism or telepathy going on?" (p. 207) when there is indication of delusions connected with thinking processes. Similarly, delusions of control of feelings, actions, and drive by external forces closely resemble beliefs in hypnotism and supernatural phenomena (e.g., poltergeists), astrology, and also religious forces. Hypnotism is now part of an accepted scientific tradition, and patients themselves not infrequently believe such "forces" to be at work. Discussing such culturally widespread beliefs with patients and relating them to psychotic phenomena, we have found, assists in destigmatizing them to the patients and their families and in laying them open to rational argument.

THE PATTERN AND STRUCTURE
OF EVERYDAY THOUGHT

The study of the pattern and structure of everyday thought also seems to have been relatively underresearched. Rachman (1983), however, has noted that

> the study of cognitive irrationality has shown that people are indeed fallible, and prone to make particular kinds of errors of reasoning. People are inclined to place disproportionate evidential value on recent events, events of personal salience, vivid events, and events that they feel

are representative. They tend to place undue emphasis on information that is easily available (to the neglect of equally or more important information which is not immediately accessible). People tend to neglect statistical data, to ignore base rates, and to express and follow inconsistent intuitions. They are capable of holding contradictory views simultaneously . . . people cannot examine directly their inferential procedures and discover their flaws; the most important personal judgments are apt to prove particularly impervious to logical insights; and people are apt to be so confident about most of their judgments that they are disinclined to examine them for the possibility of error. (p. 68)

Such findings have been demonstrated in a wide variety of "normal" populations, including groups of trained scientists (discussed further later). Various works of modern literature (beginning with James Joyce's [1922/1969] novel *Ulysses*) describe a "flow of consciousness" subject to marked variation, interruption, and distraction, and including sexual, grandiose, and paranoid matter, in a way that bears resemblance to the disordered and delusional thought of schizophrenia.

Gottesman and Shields (1982) describe some of these fleeting ideas that occur normally to individuals, but are then generally dismissed rapidly and certainly are rarely voiced to others. Although the form and content of schizophrenic thought are undoubtedly abnormal, a clearer understanding and analysis of "normal" thought form and content would seem necessary before we can firmly conclude that such abnormality is not simply an exaggeration of normality, or even an abnormal expression or persistence of thoughts common to us all.

This point is of considerable practical importance, as many patients with schizophrenia express abhorrence at the recognition that their thoughts have violent or sexual content, and see themselves as "evil" or wrong to think of such things. The expression of the distinction between thought and action can then be important therapeutically. One of our patients, for example, thought about and heard voices telling her to kill her children. In this instance, the very repulsion she felt was evidence of how little she wished to act in such a way. (It did not appear in any way, psychodynamically or otherwise, to indicate the reverse.) Explaining to her that simply thinking about an action did not mean that she had to or would act upon it appeared to reduce her anxiety and her psychotic symptoms significantly.

YOUTH CULTURE

Another major area where subcultural factors may be of importance is that of youth culture. Going to sleep in the early morning hours and wakening late—"turning night into day"—may seem a part of the schizophrenic process when it may in fact be subculturally appropriate. Misinterpretations of "evil" insignia associated with "heavy metal" rock music are easy to make. Conflict over dress, noise, and general disturbance within the family can be normal (although annoying), or perhaps it may be a nonspecific stressor contributing to the precipitation of illness. Paradoxically, however, inaccurate attribution of behavior to youthful rebelliousness rather than psychosis probably occurs frequently; when it does, it can delay appropriate intervention and prolong distress.

SHAMANISM

A final cultural perspective that may be of value to consider is that of shamanism (Tolstoy, 1985). This religious practice of great antiquity has survived to the present day in remote regions such as Siberia. Typically, as a youth, the shaman starts to behave in a strange manner and then retreats from society to live in remote isolation in the wilderness. During this period he lives entirely off the land and dresses like an animal. Frenzy is a feature, as is self-mutilation. The family members may bring a shaman who has successfully passed through this phase to support and counsel the distraught youngster. After a period of variable length, the shaman returns to the village or is brought back after a search. He appears "out of his mind" and symptoms such as auditory hallucinations and thought disorder are commonly present. Sacrifices are often made and initiation ceremonies are performed to celebrate the shaman's return to the village. The subsequent role of the shaman becomes that of mystic and prophet, whose "duties" including going into a trance, fasting, and performing the transformation of those souls in his care. Patients often find it interesting that someone who has had their symptoms in a different culture can be accorded great respect; this can help to decatastrophize the symptoms and lead to improved self-esteem.

CONCLUSIONS

Cultural considerations are important in diagnosing, understanding, and managing schizophrenia. Subcultural considerations may be important because they can be so easily overlooked and misunderstood. Not only can ideas common in society, such as ideas about the supernatural, be misinterpreted; the behavior associated with youth culture can also be misattributed in cases where it has gone beyond the bounds of normality. Exploring some of these ideas and then relating them to psychotic symptoms may be useful in helping patients to develop more appropriate thinking strategies.

Vulnerability
and Life Events

Despite the evidence we have thus far cited relating schizophrenia to normal behavior, those who are actively suffering
from it clearly differ, at least in degree, from those who are
not. Could it be that a person with schizophrenia is simply "the
wrong person, in the wrong place, at the wrong time"? Interaction between the vulnerability of the person and the life
events or circumstances he encounters seems fundamental.
Neuchterlein and colleagues (1989) recently stated that "the
general view that relationships between factors within the patient, and those in the environment, are important in understanding schizophrenia, has been widely accepted and is the
basis for vulnerability/stress models of this disorder" (p. 84). In
other words, it is generally (although still not universally)
agreed that events that happen to patients and something
about the patients themselves interact in the illness.

Neuchterlein's group has developed a tentative model of
schizophrenic episodes. The way in which information received by the senses is processed and sense made of it in the
brain (information processing) has been demonstrated to be
aberrant in many with schizophrenia, although the reason for
this has not been identified. Also, the autonomic nervous system (which controls bodily responses to stress) has been considered to be of importance in schizophrenic breakdown.
Neuchterlein et al.'s (1989) model emphasizes the mediating
role of such faulty information processing in the patient's
autonomic system, in interaction with stressful circumstances
and protective factors in the patient's environment. It is therefore a multilayered and inevitably complex model. It also im-

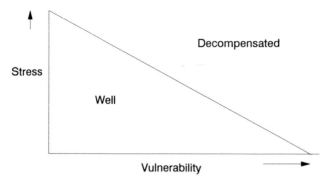

FIGURE 3.1. Vulnerability–stress interaction (after Zubin & Spring, 1977).

plies an acceptance that much as we might wish to find the cause of schizophrenia in a single event or abnormality, the likelihood is that a combination of factors is responsible.

This model builds on work by many others, but particularly Zubin and Spring (1977), who developed the concept of a vulnerability–stress diathesis (i.e., predisposition). Their hypothesis is neatly summarized by Figure 3.1. Zubin and Spring suggest that

> as long as the stress induced by challenging events stays below the threshold of vulnerability, the individual . . . remains well within the limits of normality. When the stress exceeds the threshold, the person is likely to develop a psychopathological episode of some sort . . . when the stress abates and sinks below the vulnerability threshold, the episode ends. (p. 110)

The more vulnerable the person is, the less stress is required to precipitate illness; a person with a strong family history of schizophrenia may be in this position. Conversely, those who are less vulnerable will require greater levels of stress or combination of stressors. However, other factors (to be discussed later) may interfere with the termination of episodes, so a simple reduction of stress or vulnerability is often not sufficient to enable a person to return to the previous state.

CONSTITUTIONAL VULNERABILITY

Vulnerability comprises a genetic predisposition in a sizeable proportion of those developing schizophrenia. Murray and colleagues (1988) have estimated that it contributes between 50% and 80% of the variance in the likelihood that the illness will occur. This is put in context by their comparison—"that is, of the same order as in diabetes mellitus and coronary heart disease" (p. 163). The pattern of inheritance of schizophrenia is complex and seems likely to involve a number of genes acting in concert. It is therefore unlikely that genetic counseling will have a significant impact on the illness in the short-term, any more than it has proved of any value in preventing diabetes and heart attacks.

Murray and colleagues (1988) discuss further organic factors related to the illness, including the probable effects of prenatal or perinatal injury (evidenced by the greater likelihood of being born in winter than summer in those with schizophrenia). Neuropathological signs have also been demonstrated; these include an increased size of the cerebral ventricles (cavities deep within the brain) and possible abnormalities of nerve "wiring" in the temporal lobes among a proportion of those showing signs of schizophrenia.

There is also probably a greater likelihood that those with schizoid traits will develop the illness. That is, those who tend to withdraw from social contact or remain aloof from it may be especially vulnerable. Paranoid personality traits (excessive self-reference and sensitivity) may predispose individuals to the development of psychotic symptoms as well. Murray (1984), reviewing personality and precipitants in schizophrenia, noted that "some schizophrenics give a history of long-standing personality problems and eccentricity stretching back into childhood; for example, oversensitivity and suspiciousness, odd ideas, instability, difficulties with peers and teachers" (p. 36).

However, Parnas and colleagues (1982) reviewed retrospective studies of data derived from child psychiatric agencies of children who later developed schizophrenia, and concluded that these "pre-schizophrenics only infrequently are classically withdrawn, silent personalities. Rather, they exhibit a mixture of antisocial acting-out behavior and neurotic symptoms, and at the same time have difficulties in establishing good interpersonal relationships" (p. 658). Parnas et al. noted, however, that such studies are seriously limited by selection bias, as the majority of those developing schizophrenia do not attend such agencies. They then described their own prospective longitudinal study, using controlled methodology of children of mothers with severe schizophrenia (high-risk children). Their conclusions were that in comparison with those high-risk children who did not develop schizophrenia spectrum disorders,

> those who did, were individuals who were passive babies who exhibited short attention spans. In school, they experienced interpersonal difficulties and displayed disturbing behavior, reflecting poor affective control. From clinical assessments at a mean of 15 years of age, formal disturbance and defective emotional rapport emerged as premorbid characteristics of schizophrenia spectrum disorder. . . . Furthermore, the premorbid similarity of borderline schizophrenia and schizophrenia suggests a basic relationship between these two disorders. (p. 658)

Claridge (1972) has argued from this genetic, clinical, and statistical evidence that, as we have discussed earlier, there is little support for the traditional view of "the schizophrenias" as qualitatively distinct diseases. He has suggested that they represent "in an exaggerated form, cognitive and personality characteristics found distributed among the general population" (p. 15). He suggests that the predisposition to schizophrenia has a psychophysiological basis, involving particularly the processes of arousal and attention. The appreciation that a degree of vulnerability may be manifested in premorbid (prior to illness onset) personality traits and neuropathological abnormalities is fundamental in management, because, as Zubin and Steinhauer (1981) describe,

> if premorbid adjustment was adequate, his [the patient's] return to it may be regarded as improvement or even as a cure. However a tenuous premorbid adjustment will not

be recognised as an improvement and the patient may be regarded mistakenly as still in the episode. (p. 485)

Vulnerability is a dynamic concept. Although genetic makeup and neuropathological abnormality cannot as yet be changed, personality and behavioral characteristics may be amenable to modification, such that coping abilities can be improved and resistance to precipitating factors can be built up.

LIFE EVENTS

The observation that there appears to be an interaction between events occurring in patients' lives and the onset or relapse of their illnesses has been made in regard to many psychiatric disorders, including schizophrenia. Falloon (1984) noted that "the impact of life stress on the course of schizophrenia has been observed frequently. In 1913 Emil Kraepelin remarked that remissions were often terminated by changes in the person's environment" (p. 31). The importance of such observations is that they appear to provide evidence supporting patients', relatives', and frequently therapists' beliefs that the things that happen to patients (e.g., layoff or dismissal from a job, the breakup of a marriage, a parent's death) are factors in their becoming ill. The common-sense belief seems to be that such events are important; demonstrating scientifically that this is the case has, however, proved difficult (Bebbington, et al., 1993).

Dating the onset of an illness is important in deciding whether an event is significant. Because schizophrenia frequently has a gradual, insidious onset, many studies have had to exclude more than half of patients from their analyses because onset could not be precisely dated. Events also may not occur at discrete times: For example, family arguments may be significant events but may be cumulative in effect, and moving home involves a series of traumas (e.g., buying, renting, or selling the present home, packing and unpacking) over a period of time.

Deciding whether events are independent may prove

even more difficult. For instance, was a patient dismissed from a job because he was being gradually affected by his illness and becoming less efficient, or was the dismissal quite independent of his performance? Lukoff and colleagues (1984) have comprehensively reviewed results of studies of the relationship between life events and the onset of schizophrenic episodes. After noting the methodological problems with many studies, they subdivided the research into three groups: (1) research finding significant increases in "independent" events prior to onset of acute episodes of illness, and thus suggesting that the events play a "triggering" role; (2) research finding a connection between schizoid or stress-prone patterns of living and the onset of illness; and (3) research finding no relationship.

1. *Research suggesting a "triggering" role for life events.* Life events occurring in the 3 weeks prior to the onset of symptoms were first shown to be significantly increased by Brown and Birley (1968). They also noted that long-term tension in the home appeared to increase the chances of patients' becoming disturbed after such changes. There have been replications and refinements of this work, which have developed the concept of "expressed emotion." Essentially, relapse is more likely where emotional expression—especially expression that is critical in nature—by family members toward the patient is proportionately higher. In contrast, Leff and Vaughn (1980) found that recently hospitalized patients with schizophrenia from families low in expressed emotion were significantly more likely to have experienced an independent life event in the 3 weeks preceding onset (56%) than were the patients from families high in expressed emotion (5%).

More recently, Bebbington (1990) has reported work correlating life events with computerized axial tomography (brain scan) findings in patients with schizophrenia. Preliminary results indicate that only 20% of those with brain scan abnormalities admitted to the hospital reported adverse life events, compared with 80% of those without such abnormalities. Life events were either of a lower degree insufficient to be rated, or less necessary altogether for precipitation of illness, in the more impaired and therefore presumably more vulnerable group.

2. *Research implicating schizoid or stress-prone patterns of living*. Many studies have shown an overall increase in life events prior to the onset of illness, but these have not been clearly independent. The pursuit of isolation and avoidance of social interaction appear to be continuing components of schizophrenic behavior affecting the generation of new life events. Such events may be fewer because of these avoidance strategies, but they may also be more adverse. Isolation can be a factor in the development of schizophrenia; in the opinion of many (e.g., Kay & Roth, 1961), a self-generating cycle can readily develop.

Further complications are exemplified by Brown et al.'s (1972) findings that "too enthusiastic attempts at reactivating unprepared long stay patients have been shown to lead to sudden relapse of symptoms that had not been present for years" (p. 256). Those with schizophrenia may be vulnerable to events or circumstances that are not included in standard life events interviews. Moreover, Van Putten and colleagues (1976) identified a group of patients with schizophrenia who were noncompliant with medication and "seemed to prefer psychosis to normality" (p. 1443). They correlated this with Brief Psychiatric Rating Scale scores for "grandiosity." This constitutes a further life circumstance of significance in the interaction with life events, as "some patients stop medication precisely because they prefer a schizophrenic existence" (p. 1444). Hogarty and colleagues (1973) made similar findings among the 40% of their patients who stopped medication in the first year after discharge. Patients' choices may thus complicate the dynamics of a vulnerability–stress model. Finally life events may have a multiplying effect; for example, loss of job may lead to marital conflict and precipitate separation.

3. *Research finding no relationship*. Some studies comparing patients with schizophrenia with psychiatric control groups do not report more life events in the former. However this does not exclude their contribution. Associations between life events and illness have been demonstrated to be strong in depressed patients and to occur in those with hypomania;

such associations are not, therefore, unique to schizophrenia. People seem to respond with different psychological symptoms or none at all to the same types of events, depending on their predisposition to them (both neurological and cognitive).

Of significance also is that Brown and Birley (1968), for example, had to exclude 60% of patients because of inability to date symptoms within 1 week. This inability to date onset does not exclude life events as "formative." Ongoing or cumulative difficulties or tense situations may have an attritional effect ("break the camel's back"). For example, the role of isolation in precipitating delusions without external precipitating events—for example, in deafness or blindness, or in imprisonment and consequent sensory deprivation—has been noted by Kay and Roth (1961) among others. This is, however, methodologically impossible to demonstrate at present in a definitive manner.

Lukoff and colleagues (1984) finally concluded that "stress might be a sufficient cause for some schizophrenics, a necessary cause for others, and an irrelevant factor for still others" (p. 270).

A further development of this work is the assessment of patients" levels of autonomic arousal (essentially anxiety levels), measured by skin conductance (as used in so-called "lie detectors"), in connection with their life events. Increased arousal has been demonstrated to occur when a patient is in the presence of a relative who is high in expressed emotion (Sturgeon et al., 1981). It has also been shown that there is an interaction of independent life events with the presence of a key relative (Tarrier et al., 1979).

Neuchterlein and colleagues (1989), using independent assessment of life events, confirmed previously reported work showing that independent life events are associated with autonomic arousing effects. They concluded that this is "consistent with the view that an autonomic hyperarousal state may serve as a mediating factor in exacerbating an already deteriorating environment and, unless appropriate intervention occurs, in the development of psychotic symptoms" (p. 89). Thus, they have suggested that life events may be creating anxiety, which, unless appropriate intervention occurs, may result in psychotic relapse. It would therefore seem reasonable to attempt to mitigate the effects of life events by the following practical strategies, we elaborate upon later:

1. Developing a problem-solving approach in response to the events.
2. Assessing whether the life events themselves have been accurately perceived and evaluated (i.e., taking a cognitive therapy approach to such events).
3. Enlisting appropriate social support.
4. Developing anxiety management techniques to overcome the heightened arousal.
5. Using pharmacological techniques to mitigate effects (this would include training the patient to respond with appropriate self-medication).

CONCLUSIONS

For schizophrenia to develop, it would appear to be necessary in most instances that (1) the person be vulnerable in some genetic, psychological, or physiological way; and (2) that he encounter events or circumstances in his life that affect him in a sufficiently adverse way. There are therefore two foci in management:

1. Identifying and understanding vulnerability characteristics, and then attempting whenever possible to counteract, compensate for, or modify them. (When there is no potential for modification, being able to accept and adapt to them may nevertheless be therapeutic.)
2. Identifying adverse life events and circumstances and mitigating their damaging effects, particularly by using techniques of cognitive therapy.

Suggestibility

A level of healthy skepticism in the prospective schizophrenic might be expected to militate against the acceptance of delusional beliefs and even hallucinations, but this has never been demonstrated. However, the converse has: States leading to an increased level of suggestibility seem to make the acceptance of delusions and hallucinations more likely.

CHARACTERISTICS OF ALTERED STATES: THEIR RELATION TO SUGGESTIBILITY

Suggestibility is recognized as being increased under stressful circumstances (Ludwig, 1966), and, as described in Chapter 2, under conditions of sleep and sensory deprivation. Ludwig describes "altered states of consciousness" produced by a vast assortment of situations: the variety of states previously described as causing hallucinations and delusions in normal subjects; "trance," "brainwashing," and allied states; and acute psychoses. His catalogue is lengthy, comprehensive, and well referenced. He classifies such states according to levels of stimulation, alertness, and types of motor activity (i.e., movements) involved. He then describes their general characteristics as follows:

- Alterations in thinking
- Disturbed time sense
- Loss of control
- Change in emotional expression
- Body image change
- Perceptual distortions

- Change in meaning or significance
- Sense of the ineffable
- Feelings of rejuvination
- Hypersuggestibility

Virtually all these phenomena are recognized as occurring in schizophrenia, although some, such as "feelings of rejuvenation," occur rarely. It is therefore noteworthy that they can occur in such a variety of states.

A person who is entering or in an altered state often experienced fears of losing a grip on reality and self-control ("loss of control"). Ludwig (1966) also notes that in these states, individuals show a predilection

> to attach an increased meaning or significance to their subjective experiences, ideas, or perceptions [the "change in meaning or significance" phenomenon]. . . . [The increase in meaning] is primarily an emotional or affectual experience, . . . [and] bears little resemblance to the objective "truth" of the content of this experience. (p. 229)

By "sense of the ineffable," Ludwig means that "because of the uniqueness of the subjective experience . . . persons claim a certain ineptness or inability to communicate the nature or essence of the experience to someone who has not undergone a similar experience" (p. 229). This may be of considerable significance in explaining some of the recognized difficulties in establishing a rapport with patients with schizophrenia: They may well feel that they cannot tell others about experiences that they perceive to be unique. Being able to demonstrate empathy, provide a rationale, and describe how others can recognize such experiences may therefore be of fundamental importance.

The "hypersuggestibility" of individuals in altered states may be of importance in the development of delusions, as Ludwig notes: "With the recession of a person's critical faculties there is an attendant decrease in his capacity for reality testing or his ability to distinguish between subjective and objective reality" (p. 230). This may lead to misinterpretation, but it may also mean that appropriate intervention, while the person remains in this acute state, can be effective at counter-acting errors in reality testing. This may particularly be the case when the person tends

> to create the compensatory need to bolster up his failing faculties by seeking out certain props, support, or guid-ance in an effort to relieve some of the anxiety associated with this loss of control. In his attempt to compensate for his failing critical faculties, the person comes to rely more on the suggestions of the . . . shaman, . . . interrogator, . . . preacher or doctor, all representing omnipotent author-itative figures. (p. 230)

The potential for both positive and negative influence, therefore, would appear to be considerable. Ludwig discusses various functions of these states, both maladaptive (as in psychosis) and adaptive (including potential healing proper-ties, avenues of new knowledge or experience, and social func-tions). He expresses the quite reasonable belief that "it . . . [is] difficult to accept that, for example, man's ability to lapse into a trance has been evolved just so he can be hypnotized on stage or in a clinical or laboratory setting" (pp. 230–231). Being able to express the positive attributes of these states of hypersug-gestibility may be of some benefit with some patients, partic-ularly after recovery from an acute episode.

As mentioned in Chapter 3, it is well recognized that isolation acts as a vulnerability agent in schizophrenia (Kay & Roth, 1961). Suggestibility may be more likely to operate ne-gatively when a person feels unable to discuss matters of con-cern with a confidant. His relationship with his parents, from whom he may be separating, may have deteriorated or may never have been close. Close relationships outside the family may never have developed or may not be available because of personal characteristics or circumstances (e.g., moving to a different town or foreign country to work or study). Even in a case where communication can occur within such a relation-ship, the partner's or parents' beliefs or way of communicating them may sometimes be so abnormal as to confuse the person further rather than enlighten him. Criticism, known to be of significance in relapse (Leff & Vaughn, 1980), tends to lead to further isolation and breakdown in communication ("Nobody understands; they are all against me").

CONCLUSIONS

Suggestibility may be of importance in the development of delusional beliefs. Stressful circumstances heightening suggestibility have been described as frequently coinciding with the onset of schizophrenia. At such times, the ascribing of inappropriate significance and inaccurate implications to nonthreatening events may be an important step in the development of a psychotic illness.

Thinking

Disturbance of thinking is central to schizophrenia. Schizophrenic thought disorder is not a unitary deficit, but has several components (Cutting & Murphy, 1988):

1. *Disorder of the content of thinking.* The subject matter of thought is frequently abnormal in schizophrenia, as demonstrated by delusions and overvalued ideas.

2. *Disorder of the mechanism of thinking* (alternatively described as "intrinsic thinking disturbance"). The process of thinking is disturbed. Four of the best-known such features of schizophrenia are the following:

a. *Loosening of associations.* The links between succeeding thoughts seem to be broken or at least tenuous. The normal flow of thinking seems disrupted.

b. *Concrete thinking.* Abstract thought seems to be lacking. For example, a person with schizophrenia may explain a proverb (e.g., "A rolling stone gathers no moss") in terms of the objects and material concepts described ("A stone which goes down a hill doesn't rub any moss off on it").

c. *Overinclusion.* Thoughts are not focused and include material that is not apparently relevant.

d. *Illogicality and irrational reasoning.*

3. *Disorder of the way thoughts are expressed.* This is usually called "formal (i.e., pertaining to form) thought disorder"; however, because it is essentially a disorder of language affecting conversational discourse, Cutting and Murphy (1988) have suggested that it would be better described as a "conversational abnormality."

4. *Disorder of the way events in the real world are thought about*

or judged. This is deficient real-world knowledge, or a relative "lack of common sense." This is a concept developed by Cutting and Murphy (1988), with major practical implications that we describe in detail later.

DELUSIONS

The concept of "delusions" has received remarkably little critical analysis, given its profound significance to psychiatric practice (Roberts, 1992). Delusions may be described as irrational beliefs that are out of keeping with a person's cultural (or socioeconomic) background and that are not amenable to reason; or, alternatively, as beliefs (probably false) that are held in spite of evidence to the contrary and that are out of keeping with the person's social, cultural, educational, or religious background. Each part of either definition involves dynamic concepts, which in turn involve judgments being made by those determining whether the person is deluded or not.

"Irrational" or "probably false" is dependent on the assessor's understanding of the person's mode of thinking (see the later description of the application of Piaget's work to this area). It is also determined by the assessor's appreciation of the person's culture (see Chapter 2), which may be much more difficult than seems currently to be appreciated. As discussed there, we and other mental health professionals in Britain are now more likely to recognize the significance of Afro-Caribbean culture in relation to the presentation of psychiatric symptoms. We are also more likely to recognize the subcultural influences of "charismatic" Christianity or religious sects. However, we may fail to appreciate the subtleties and prevalence of, for example, beliefs in the supernatural or fantasy, or to understand the precise meaning of words used idiomatically or as part of a local dialect. Youth cultures ("heavy metal," "skins," etc.) change so rapidly that terms become outdated and are replaced by others; this too can lead to misunderstanding and influence "delusion detection" markedly.

Subcultural context can also be of some importance in

understanding the specific nature and form of a delusion. For example, a patient described "a silicon chip inside my head"; this followed a suicide attempt resulting in a head injury in 1982, and the specific term appeared to have arisen from a pop song ("I Don't Like Mondays" by Bob Geldof and the Boomtown Rats) that was current at the time. One line in the song states, "The silicon chip inside my head is moved to overload." Although it might seem unlikely that any song could be of major influence in delusion formation, this particular one was of emotional significance, because it was written after a scholar in the United States shot a number of schoolmates in what was regarded as an incomprehensible crime, and stated that he did it because he disliked Monday mornings.

The usual safeguard applied to reduce such cultural confusion is to consult members of the individual's culture. However, this requires, first, recognition that cultural factors are relevant, and second, determination of who exactly are members of the individual's culture. Parents may be, but frequently cultural differences with parents are cited as a factor in the person's problematical situation ("They don't understand me"). Friends from the person's peer group can be of considerable assistance, but often concerns over confidentiality or even "culture clash" with the assessor can lead to their being excluded. In practice, it may be that a junior member of the therapeutic team, a visiting student, a member of the ward support staff, or some other individual of similar background and of like mind will be best able to establish a relationship. This individual can then mediate with other members of the team and even explain the significance in context of apparently delusional material.

That delusions are not amenable to reason is held to be self-evident: "Neither previous experience nor compelling counter-arguments can shake the certainty of the delusion" (Scharfetter, 1980, p. 150). However, few controlled investigations using appropriate rating instruments have been performed to establish this to be the case, and these few studies (e.g., Watts et al., 1973; Milton et al., 1978) have suggested that the contrary can occur: Delusions seem to be held with

differing degrees of intensity and to last for varying lengths of time. One might anticipate that whether they are amenable to reason will depend on the following factors (see Figure 5.1):

1. *The strength of the belief.* This may be in part related to the time period over which the belief has been present.

2. *The consequences of relinquishing the belief.* Increased social acceptability may be a reason for giving up a belief, whereas investment of self-esteem may militate against it. For example, when a patient has acted in accordance with paranoid or grandiose beliefs over many years, he may have forsaken or not developed a career, marriage, and/or family and may have faced ridicule because of the beliefs. The effects on his self-esteem of admitting he was wrong at a late stage may be a factor in his continuing to hold them, although he may discontinue acting upon them.

3. *The joint discovery of alternative explanations.* This will depend, in part, on the depth of the therapist's understanding of the beliefs and their antecedents. It will also be determined

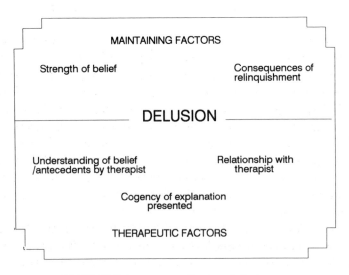

FIGURE 5.1. Factors affecting delusions.

by the therapist's ability to develop pertinent strategies in appropriate sequence, and the persistence to follow through with them.

4. *The way in which the explanations are presented.* Milton and colleagues (1978) produced some evidence that attempts at modification rather than direct confrontation seemed more likely to be successful.

5. *The relationship with the therapist.* The person may well be more likely to accept the arguments of someone who is trusted and respected.

"Delusional perception" is of diagnostic importance in schizophrenia and as such requires separate consideration. It is generally defined as the attachment of a private meaning to a consensually validated phenomenon. Schneider (1973) has defined it as occurring in cases where

> abnormal significance [is] attached to a real percept without any cause that is understandable in rational or emotional terms. This abnormal significance tends mostly towards self-reference. . . . Delusional perception is not the same as investing an experience with abnormal significance for some reason. We need not concern ourselves with misinterpretations or errors of reasoning for which there is an understandable, rational cause. (p. 33)

He does not, however, describe how we are expected to differentiate these latter (i.e., misinterpretations) from the former (delusional perceptions). Although a categorical definition is presented, the elaboration begins to suggest a continuum, which Schneider's further discussion of "delusional intuitions" reinforces. He describes these as "sudden delusional ideas, such as a summons from God, ideas of special powers, of persecution, of being loved" (p. 34). He adds that "there is no conceptual difference between them and the sudden compulsive thoughts and 'overvalued' ideas which occur to non-psychotics" (p. 34).

Schneider (1973) nevertheless continues to imply a clear division between delusional perception, which cannot be understood, and delusional intuition and normal belief, which can be. He gives an example:

> To a person not suffering from a delusion two crossed
> pieces of wood, if he notices them at all, are nothing but a
> pattern made out of two pieces of wood. To a schizophren-
> ic they may mean more, indicating perhaps that he will be
> crucified. (p. 35)

Although Schneider presents this as a clear contrast, one
might postulate that the symbolism of the cross (especially with
pieces of wood) is too widely known to go unrecognized by all
people who do not have schizophrenia, and that intermediate
positions between delusional perception and no significance
may be as likely to be taken. He later says that delusional
perceptions and intuitions may be "supernatural in nature, as
if they come from 'another dimension'" (p. 37). Belief in supernatural phenomena has previously been described as
much commoner than, in strict scientific terms, we might wish
it to be, and religious or magical significance may be readily
attached to otherwise innocuous occurrences. Schneider's further discussion can again be taken to reinforce the concept of
a continuum between psychotic and normal thinking:

> It is not unusual for a non-psychotic person to have a
> symbolic perceptual experience which is reminiscent of
> delusional perception. For example, someone is walking
> along a street, the street lamp goes out, and it suddenly
> comes into his mind that his sweetheart has had an acci-
> dent. . . . We are dealing with a different kind of experi-
> ence for it is not "without cause," since the interpretation
> is understandable in terms of the person's prevailing
> mood, which is at least one of mild, private concern. . . .
> Isolated symbolic experiences of this kind, therefore, in
> our view come within the delusion-like reactions which
> are of common occurrence . . . there is, moreover, no trace
> of personal involvement by a "higher reality." (p. 36)

When such an involvement is believed to have taken place,
deviation from reality into psychosis has generally occurred by
definition, although even this is complicated by religious belief. Schneider's evidence would therefore appear to be supportive of the opposite position to the one he initially pro-

poses—that is, that normal experience overlaps with psychotic experiences.

Perhaps creative inspiration may occupy an intermediary position. Reed (1970) has noted that

> many creative people (writers, painters, and scientists alike) report the suddenness with which original ideas come to them. . . . [The novelist] Dorothy Canfield describes how her creative work begins with a heightened emotional awareness during which any chance event, insignificant in itself (an expression, a fragment of conversation) may be the germ from which a story may grow, a description surprisingly reminiscent of *Wahnstimmung* [delusional mood] . . . and the development of primary delusions. (p. 20)

He adds:

> [The poet A. E.] Housman tells how . . . parts of a poem would come spontaneously into his mind, something he found beyond his control and which, although in a way pleasant, was also agitating, exhausting and at times embarrassing. . . . There are similarities here to the self reports of feelings of loss of control of thought with accompanying emotional disturbance given by schizophrenics. (p. 135)

Jacobs (1980) provides a conceptualization of the development of primary delusions from a cognitive perspective, which initially refers to Jaspers"s description of

> how prior to the genesis of delusions, the person feels uncanny. Gross uncertainty drives him instinctively to look for some fixed point to which he can cling. The sudden consciousness of an idea, even though false, immediately has a soothing, strengthening and euphoric effect. (pp. 556–557)

This delusional mood, represented as feelings of panic, perplexity, fear, and strangeness in which the person may feel alienated, different, and isolated, is relieved by the feeling of certainty that the primary delusion provides. Jacobs suggests that in the "lucid delusional schizophrenic the ability to me-tathink [that is, think about one's thinking] is grossly impaired or absent" (p. 559), and that whereas normally thinking precedes knowing, in this instance the reverse occurs. However, it may be simply that the reassurance of finding a meaningful explanation, however improbable, in a frenetically distressing and perplexing situation is sufficient to explain why the delusion is reached for and clung to so energetically.

Arthur (1964) has suggested that "a delusion thus is a premature closure, a kind of dogmatic interpretation of events" (p. 107). Jacobs (1980) then proceeds to describe possible "delusiogenic schemata" (p. 559), which may be acquired early in development and predispose an individual to delusions in later life. Although it is difficult to confirm the existence of such predisposing schemata, the principle of attempting to understand the global assumptions that are present prior to the onset of delusional ideas is clearly important. These may in turn be traced back. The assessor may ask simply, "You seem to have been feeling that people were against you. What circumstances led you to that conclusion?" or "What made you think that?" Being bullied at school, deserted by a partner, or the like and particularly a combination of such events, may have been significant in the formation of paranoid or depressive schemata. Feeling undervalued or being taken for granted may also contribute to grandiose or depressive schemata.

Jacobs (1980) makes the point that the development of a relationship in which sufficient trust prevails is essential to prevent the therapist from being included among those in the patient's delusional pseudocommunity who are intent on doing him harm. It is then "recommended that the patient be helped to remember the primary delusional experience . . . in all its emotional, perceptual, and cognitive aspects. . . . the patient is made aware of how he leaped away from his overwhelming uncertainties into delusional knowing" (p. 562).

In summary, it would therefore seem reasonable to suppose that "irrational" thoughts occur normally but are usually corrected, rather than persisting or being elaborated into delusional beliefs. In delusional perception, these are thoughts to which inappropriate significance is attached. Momentary thoughts of this kind appear to be of common occurrence. The persistence of such thoughts may be the crucial element in schizophrenia, rather than their nature. Reasons why such persistence occurs can be postulated; for example, neuropsychological deficit, isolation, and/or stress may create or increase suggestibility, as discussed previously. Such reasons may be useful in tentative explanations to the patient, but it is crucial that they should not detract from attempts to modify such delusional beliefs. Philosophers such as Ayer (1964) express doubts about the very nature of "one's experience of other minds." Perhaps we need to be more skeptical about our ability to decide that such minds are intractably deluded.

INTRINSIC THINKING DISTURBANCE

To understand intrinsic thinking disturbance in schizophrenia, it is pertinent to review and compare the development of thinking processes in "normal" people and patients. The Swiss biologist and child psychologist Jean Piaget's description of the development of thinking processes in children (e.g., Piaget, 1929/1973) has gained widespread acceptance. Tissot and Burnand (1980) have described the application of Piaget's "genetic psychology" and the tests he developed to schizophrenia.

Piaget's approach is biological and genetic in the sense of going back to the beginning of the development of thinking in the child. Children's thinking is recognized as not simply being that of scaled-down, miniature "rational/scientific" adults, but as quite different in kind with different stages of development. Piaget saw intelligence as adaptation to the environment, which, when achieved, produces a state of equilibrium between the actions of the individual and the actions of the environment. The child adapts to the environment by taking in (assimilating) incoming information, and then accommodating to it.

Piaget also spoke of "schema" as an "inferred element of that cognitive, structural organisation responsible for shaping and recurrence of the actions of an organism" (Wright et al., 1970, p. 499). Schemata, in other words, are organizing processes that allow information to be made sense of, and affect the actions of the individual. However, because they have this shaping function, they impose a structure that may also be distorting or at least oversimplifying. This is similar, to the way in which this term is used in cognitive therapy, although perhaps broader in scope.

Piaget proposed four main stages in the development of thinking processes:

1. *Sensorimotor* (0–2 years). Sensation and movement predominate at this stage.

2. *Preconceptual thought* (2–7 years).

a. *Symbolic thought.* Acquisition of play and language is occurring.

b. *Intuitive thought.* Some characteristics of this stage resemble textbook descriptions of the patient with schizophrenia:

> The child's use of language and his thinking are egocentric. ... Since words have been assimilated to a private, even idiosyncratic symbolic function, the child is, to a considerable extent, attaching private meanings to public signs and is unaware of the fact; for his social experience is not yet rich enough for him to realise that others do not share his private meanings. (Wright et al., 1970, p. 506)

This closely resembles the development of delusional perceptions described earlier.

3. *Concrete operations* (7–11 years). The child at this stage still lacks abstract thought. Reciprocity (being able to take into account the views of others) develops, but Piaget believed this to be very dependent on interaction with other children.

4. *Formal operations* (11 years and above). At this stage, reasoning by hypothesis and deduction of consequences develops, and it is the development of this stage that Tissot and Burnand (1980) have particularly investigated.

One criticism of Piaget's work has been that problems have arisen with the age ranges given, as children's development varies beyond the ranges given. Piaget accepted that this range of variability is wide, but he believed the basic sequence to be correct. Effects of training and culture were also initially ignored to a large extent; he did later recognize their importance.

Dulit (1972) and Niemark (cited in Wright et al., 1970) found that only about a third of adults and older children do in fact reach the stage of formal-operational thought. They concluded that formal-operational tasks are not mastered more or less simultaneously, or even by a majority of people. Again, a continuum in experimental, scientific thinking appears to be present. This is of great importance in questioning the assumption that "normal" thinking is rational and scientific; thinking in a majority of the population appears to be at a much more concrete level most of the time.

Hemsley and Garety (1986) describe ways in which recent work on the formation of normal beliefs may aid understanding of delusional thinking. Establishment of delusions may result from abnormal perceptual or other anomalous experiences with the process by which they are formed may be the same as that occuring in the development of normal beliefs. Two factors appear significant: prior expectation shaping belief formation, and the current relevant information provided by the environment. Hemsley and Garety then discuss similarities in the maintenance of "normal" an abnormal beliefs. They note that "normal" strongly held beliefs are highly resistant to change and that information incongruent with them tends to be disregarded; this also occurs with delusional thought, by definition.

Hemsley and Garety (1986) then describe a "Bayesian analysis" of delusional beliefs, based on the work of Fischoff and Bayeth-Marom (1983). This formulates knowledge in terms of statements or hypotheses, each of which is characterized by a subjective probability, which should then be revised in the light of new information. They describe how potential biases can occur at different stages of hypothesis evaluation:

1. *Hypothesis formulation.* Although seemingly essential, this initial stage may not occur at all. This is rare in normal subjects, but it occurs traditionally in schizophrenia. That is, it is suggested that patients appear at times to translate abnormal experiences directly into belief statements without any intervening stage of considering evidence. Alternatively, the beliefs developed may be untestable—for example, "that the world will end in the year 2093."

2. *Assessing component probabilities.* Errors in summation of probability may occur. For example, a subject may express 100% confidence that the Irish Republican Army is plotting against him, but also a one-in-five chance that no such plot exists. This is also recognized as a component of normal belief. Similarly, overreliance on the availability and representativeness of the data used occurs frequently. A young paranoid patient treated by Hemsley and Garety was preoccupied by his appearance, and as a result felt that 80% of people were laughing at him. Accompanied by the therapist on a walk, he established a score of 15% for those simply smiling, not necessarily at him.

3. *Assessing prior odds.* Subjects may act as though a hypothesis is absolutely true, without having seriously considered the possibility that it might not be. Although this is seemingly unlikely, it is not uncommon in clinical practice, and evidence can be weighed with the patient supporting the converse beliefs to the ones held.

4. *Assessing the likelihood ratio.* People can interpret and reinterpret new information so as to render it consistent with their previously held beliefs.

5. *Information search.* Some deluded patients report no information search at all. With delusional perception, patients frequently describe how they have no need for any confirming or disconfirming evidence because of the certainty of the initial experience. In cases where searching does occur, patients usually restrict the search to confirmatory evidence.

6. *Action.* The relationship between belief and action is far from simple; believing that something is true does not inevitably lead to acting as if it were true. There is a considerable literature on the willingness of individuals to stake money on

their beliefs. Generally subjects are far more cautious in deed than word. Deluded patients frequently appear to act in ways inconsistent with their beliefs.

Brett-Jones et al. (1987) describe five dimensions of delusion that can be useful in assessing change (see items 1–5 in Table 5.1). In using the scale with deluded patients they noted that for most patients, there did not appear to be an active process of reality testing of the relevant beliefs. Disconfirmatory experiences did not often arise, and most patients did not go out and search for them. When they were active in considering evidence for and against a belief, they were much more likely to be aware of hallucinatory experiences that confirmed their delusions than of objective experiences that were disconfirmatory. However, this is not unlike what occurs in the formation of normal belief, suggesting that it may be only the content rather than the process of formation of delusional belief that distinguishes it from normality. As Brett-Jones et al. remark, "It may be the very complexity of delusions . . . that has made researchers wary of attempting to undertake empirical studies" (p. 265).

Tissot and Burnand (1980) found intelligence quotients to be below average in their group with schizophrenia. This was not due to loss of operation of the intellect but due to difficulty in "actualising the operations"—that is, using abstract thought. Their study's "objective . . . [was therefore] to grasp the structure of their reasoning and its integration with reality. Clinical experience does not suggest that the reasoning structure of schizophrenics is impaired [but that] they no longer utilise [it]" (p. 657). The persons with schizophrenia were found to have greatest difficulty in the area of formal operations described as "logico-experimental reasoning." This involves assimilation of new evidence and reasoning abstractly on the basis of it. Therefore, cognitive and behavioral techniques that focus on reasoning, hypothesis testing, and problem solving may address these specific deficits. Tissot and Burnand's final conclusion, as quoted in Chapter 2, was that "when rational explanations and the certainty they produce [are] lacking, magical causality and subjective certainty take

TABLE 5.1. Summary of Scales and Categories

Score	Conviction[a] (6-point ordinal)	Preoccupation[a] (6-point ordinal)	Interference (4-point ordinal)	Reaction to hypothetical contradiction (Categorical)	Accommodation (Categorical)
0	Do not believe	—	0 None at al	Situation ignored, dismissed, or persistently denied as being possible	No instance given or something mentioned, but with no effect of belief
1	I doubt that ...	I think about these things not at all ...	1 Incidences given of minor changes (e.g., smoked a cigarette, unable to touch something)	Situation accommodated into the belief system by some alteration such that belief and situation are now consistent	Some alteration in the content of the belief, but no change in any of measures of interest or belief replaced directly by new belief
2	I have a few doubts that ...	... occasionally	2 Disruption to normal hospital routine (e.g., unable to go to occupational therapy not eating meals)	Belief changes in conviction but not in content	A change in conviction but with no change in content
3	I feel fairly sure that ...	... some of the time	3 Severe disruption to normal activities (e.g., violent behavior, not able to leave one room)	Belief dropped in the face of contradictory evidence	The belief has been dropped with no replacement, and the subject attributes this to some objective event
4	I believe very strongly that ...	... most of the time	4 —	—	
5	I know/I am absolutely certain that ...	... absolutely all the time			A change in preoccupation or interference, but with no change in content

Note. From Brett-Jones et al. (1987). Copyright 1987 by the British Psychological Society. Reprinted by permission.

[a]Scores on these two scales fall between two verbal descriptions; for example a score of 1 on conviction implies that the subject responded that they were *more* certain than the card which stated "I doubt that ... (statement of belief)" and that they were *less* certain than the card which stated "I have a few doubts that ...."

their place" (p. 663). This powerfully portrays the outcome of thought disorder and the targets for cognitive therapies.

Harrow and Prosen (1978) took a different perspective on thought disorder, examining the significance of the content disclosed. They proposed that intermingling of material from the past or current experience of people who have schizophrenia occurs in their speech. A total of 30 young (average age = 22) people with schizophrenia were interviewed within 2 weeks of hospitalization.

1. During the acute stage of the disorder, the patients were given specific standardized test material in the form of proverbs and social comprehension questions. Eight responses from each patient were selected for subsequent inquiry.

2. The following week, a psychiatrist conducted a standardized tape-recorded interview with each patient to detect the reasons for these responses.

3. Afterwards, members of the research team used the taped interviews to rate the patients' responses for their idiosyncratic responses along a number of standardized dimensions. These included whether or not the bizarre responses were influenced by the patients' intermingling material from their past or current experiences, and whether or not the responses were influenced by disordered logic.

Harrow and Prosen's results demonstrated intermingling occurring in 80% of the patients to some degree, but disordered logic was more unusual (in 24%, with only 7% to a severe degree). When the idiosyncratic, bizarre, or "autistic" responses were examined closely and the tapes under discussion were explored more carefully with the patients, it became clear that there was a rationale for the inappropriate material that had been intermingled into their responses. Of those who intermingled material, over 90% were rated as producing material related in some way to their personal lives. It did not incidentally, appear to arise from "primitive drive material" of a sexual or aggressive nature, as suggested by Freudian theory.

Logical reasoning, it was suggested, may be a problem in

a more chronic population, but it was not a very significant one in this group. The experimenters raised the question as to why a person with schizophrenia does not edit out idiosyncratic verbalizations: Is he incapable of recognizing them and/or of editing them? Although this question is of theoretical importance and worthy of further investigation, the practical finding of major significance—confirming clinical impression and much anecdotal evidence—is that what patients say has meaning to them even when they are thought-disordered. We describe an example of such intermingling in thought disorder later in this book (Turkington & Kingdon, 1991—expanded in Part II as Study 4); in this case, the patient responded to cognitive therapy.

Kaney and Bentall (1989) looked at persecutory delusions and attributional style—that is, who or what patients tended to attribute to, or hold responsible for, events occurring to them. They found that their psychotic patients with persecutory delusions made excessively external attributions for negative events, and internal attributions for positive events in comparison with controls. They were thus more likely to ascribe control of negative events externally to others, and positive events to themselves. This suggests a fundamental error in their general perception of the control of events. The delusional patients also showed significant differences pertaining to beliefs in magical forces (they were more likely to believe in them), which relates to the work cited earlier by Tissot and Bernand (1980).

FORMAL THOUGHT DISORDER

Reed (1970) has comprehensively reviewed studies of schizophrenic thought disorder. He has concluded that "much of what is found in schizophrenic thought, speech and writing also occurs in normal people" (p. 22). He notes that "both Kraepelin and Bleuler believed that schizophrenic thought was similar to the thought of normal people during dreams" (p. 4). Carl Schneider, according to Reed, believes that irrelevancy is the dominant disorder of thinking and compares this to "the type of thinking . . . found in normal people during extreme fatigue or in the hypnagogic state" (p. 4).

Reed (1970) describes work demonstrating "extreme intellectual slowness" in people with schizophrenia, since established as "attentional–perceptual deficit" (see, e.g., Brenner, 1989). He reports that

> in an everyday situation, because of their slowness, schizophrenics might not have the time to think out the answer to one problem before the next presented, and a way of handling this handicap would be to answer at random or to give the obvious answer even if it were incorrect. This would give the appearance of thought disorder. . . . Kurt Schneider emphasizes the normality of much that is considered pathognomonic of schizophrenia. Thought blocking is considered a universal and non-specific phenomenon occurring frequently in shy and embarrassed people or in profound depression. "Disjointed," "fragmented" and "inconsequent" thinking with apparently inadequate connection between thoughts although a "common fashion of speech and thought" in schizophrenia also occurs to a lesser degree in normals, those who are "scatter-brained" and "inconsequential" either in normal circumstances or when drunk or in emotional turmoil. (p. 7)

Reed then, as mentioned earlier, discusses work on the relationship between creativity and thinking:

> Much . . . of what we call abnormal in schizophrenic speech and writing both in form and production may be found in creative work. . . . in the same way that close study of schizophrenic speech enables one to understand something of its meaning and how it comes to be formed, so may study of obscure poetry make its meaning clearer. (p. 18)

He illustrates this with poetry by e. e. cummings and Dylan Thomas, and then notes that

> it seems we may coin new words or fashions of speech for new inventions and experiences yet deem this abnormal

for schizophrenics who suffer a multitude of new experiences and have a need as Kraepelin says for "expressions
of more complicated or morbid ideas for which no words
exist." (pp. 21–22)

Again, there seems evidence of a continuum between normal and schizophrenic thought. The characteristics of the
schizophrenic extreme of this continuum—thought block,
perseveration, flight of ideas, derailment, and circumstantial
thinking—are frequently encountered in clinical practice, yet
little specific guidance is available as to how they should be
managed. They seem to be initially worsened by discussion of
emotionally significant or stressful topics, or confrontation
even over simple domestic matters. However, a continued
gentle focus on emotional themes may lead to increasing lu-
cidity.

Bannister (Dryden, 1985) describes how he has formu-
lated this dilemma about how to respond to thought disorder
and delusional talk or beliefs: "by this I mean that the client
will talk at length in a manner which is extremely puzzling and
extremely difficult to relate to, in a sense claiming things which
you cannot accept as true" (p. 168). He notes that one classic
way of responding is to humour the patient: "You pretend to
agree that the client does have, for example, magical powers
in his fingertips. . . . You go along, you pretend to agree, you
smile and say 'yes' and you say 'how dreadful' " (p. 168). He
suggests, however, that although this may help the therapist
get along with the patient,

> I think, in the long run, it is quite dangerous for the client
> because it leaves him without any landmarks. . . . if every-
> thing [the client says] is going to be agreed with, [he has]
> no way of finding out whether particular points of view
> make any more sense to people than others. (pp. 168–169)

Another way Bannister describes of responding is "rational argument": "It not only seems the sensible thing to
do—not to put up with this nonsense—but it also seems that
you are doing a kindness by arguing with the patient" (p. 169).

However, he describes the difficulties he has found with this approach. He notes that "the client is not only saying things you find it hard to believe but also [has] different notions of evidence and a different kind of logical assessment of evidence coming from you." He then describes selectively ignoring delusional or thought-disordered talk as a strategy; however, he has found that this creates an artificial relationship that does not transfer to situations outside the hospital, where workmates and others do not ignore such talk.

Bannister's final preferred way of working is to start dealing with the theme of the delusions rather than their content. He describes an example of a patient who had elaborate paranoid ideas about his doctors. By discussing the nature of the relationship he had with his doctors, rather than the content of the delusions, Bannister managed successfully to engage and work with him.

In a case where a patient is apparently not thinking at all ("thought blocking"), there is also little textbook guidance about how one should proceed. Should one await a response, divert the patient's attention, or interpret one's perception of the patient's mental state to him? Should one ask whether or suggest that the patient may be hallucinating, or simply losing the "thread of thought" (as Reed, 1970, mentions occurring in a much more transient way in anxiety)?

With perseveration and circumstantial thinking, it would seem reasonable to use conventional cognitive therapy techniques, such as focusing on targeted agenda items and discussing topics that are not emotionally arousing (such as those that will have been garnered by diary keeping or recall of daily events). Again, belief modification rather than confrontation (Milton et al., 1978) may be the approach of choice. Recognition of emotionally significant areas and a graduated approach to discussion of problematic areas or themes as Bannister describes, over a period of months or even years rather than hours or days, may be appropriate. Total avoidance of such areas would seem to reinforce the possible use of thought disorder as a defense. Some patients appear to make conscious use of thought disorder in these circumstances, or at least health professionals frequently think this to be the case.

Whether or not this is so, the use of confrontation, so fre-
quently invoked, would seem likely to be counterproductive.
Reinforcement of positive behavior has been demonstrated
(Hemsley, 1986) to be of some effect in these circumstances.

DEFICIENCIES IN REAL-WORLD KNOWLEDGE

Bizarre expressions are quite frequent in schizophrenia and
are often the reason used by nonprofessionals for deeming a
person "crazy." However, their very imprecise and variable
nature makes them of little use in psychiatric diagnosis, and
investigation of their nature has been correspondingly neglected. The major exception to this has been the work of
Cutting and Murphy (1988), who have recently proposed that
patients with schizophrenia have a disorder of the way they
think about or judge events in the real world; this is described
as deficient real-world knowledge or "lack of common sense."
The authors give an example of a patient who had been hospitalized for 27 years. He expressed the belief that he was still
suffering from flu or pneumonia that he had caught from a
thermometer in the hospital at the start of his illness.

This and other bizarre notions about the real world, Cutting and Murphy suggest, could be described as delusions;
however, this stretches the term to include any bizarre statement about the world, whether it is a strongly held belief or
not. One could also argue that this signifies an intrinsic
thought disturbance—that is, an inability to follow logical inferences, or overinclusive categorisation (including thermom-
eters as disease causes rather than as measures of a disease
process). The authors' alternative to these conventional responses, however, is to suggest a breakdown or gap in knowledge of the real world. They suggest that knowledge itself is
deficient, rather than that the thinking process itself is abnormal.

Cutting and Murphy investigated the frequency of all the
types of thought disorder described above in 20 people with
schizophrenia and in 30 controls with depression or neurotic
disorders (matched for intelligence and sex). Two tests of real-

world knowledge were devised, one covering practical and the other social knowledge, and these were standardized on normal subjects (in this instance, members of the hospital staff). They found that one-quarter of the patients with schizophrenia in an acute episode had definite intrinsic disturbance of thinking. However, three-quarters were markedly deficient in their knowledge of everyday social issues.

The practical implications of this finding are considerable. We could attempt to improve such knowledge of everyday issues directly, and it is possible that this may be one of the mechanisms by which social skills training (as described, e.g., by Trower et al., 1978) in this group is effective. We could also isolate specific areas of deficit and focus attention upon them.

One example of how this can be done arose in our retrospective series of patients (Kingdon & Turkington, 1991a) and is described in more detail later (see Part II, Study 2). A patient presented to us saying that he was frightened that the moon, which was full at the time, might fall on the flat where he lived alone. This was taken at face value and treated as a specific educational deficit relating to an ignorance of the way in which gravitational and rotational forces keep the moon rotating around the earth. He accepted this explanation when it was given, remained in the hospital overnight only, and then returned to his flat. On questioning a number of years later, we have found that he continues to accept the explanation, and has reached the stage where he can find it amusing that he ever believed otherwise.

CONCLUSIONS

Although consideration of the form and content of thought is central to any discussion of schizophrenia, assumptions have been made about some key concepts, especially delusions, that are probably inappropriate. We have described how deciding whether someone is deluded is a complex judgment based not just on the cultural but the subcultural background of both the person and his assessor. Whether beliefs are amenable to reason depends on many variables, including the skill of the therapist in leading the patient to review evidence, and also the quality of the therapist's relationship with the patient.

Thought disorder seems not to be as arbitrary as it at first appears. It may relate to abnormalities in logico-experimental reasoning, idiosyncratic intermingling of personally significant material, and deficiencies in real-world knowledge. Focusing on the themes of conversation may be a more useful way of tackling thought disorder than discussing the specific content presented.

Communication

Disturbances of speech are one of the most obvious signs in schizophrenia. Their effect on the individual is to isolate him from others, which will secondarily reinforce his disabling symptoms. He will be less able and likely to communicate his beliefs, and thus to subject them to the critical analysis of relatives, friends, and public opinion. The regular feedback of others, which shapes opinion, attitude and belief will be restricted or even abolished, and so abnormal beliefs may proliferate and solidify. Speech disturbances may also specifically increase paranoid preoccupation, because the perceived communication difficulty and the "strange looks" the person receives as a result of bizarre speech may be misinterpreted as threatening.

Most psychopathologists have regarded such disturbances as an indication of underlying disorder of thought. However, a review by Wykes (1980) of language disturbance notes that some authors have proposed specific abnormalities in the use of language, in addition to such thought disorder. Their supposition has been that people with schizophrenia are deficient in their ability to utilize the syntactic (essentially grammatical) and semantic (related to meaning) constraints of language. However, the abnormalities may have arisen from the lack of direct comparison of schizophrenic speech patterns with normal speech production. Wykes and others (e.g., Argyle, 1978) also cite evidence that the speech errors demonstrated are "not unique to schizophrenics; not only are they produced by normal speakers . . . but they are also produced by previous personnel of the White House" (Wykes, 1980, p. 403). Imprecise or simply inaccurate use of language is not uncommon, particularly when a person is nervous and in-articulate.

"TAKING THE ROLE OF THE OTHER"

Wykes (1980) goes on to review evidence suggesting that although people with schizophrenia may be good listeners, they may not be good at communicating. She cites work demonstrating that appropriate sequencing of sentences and cohesive links between them are more likely to be missing. This means that schizophrenic conversation is more difficult to follow than is normally the case.

Rutter (1985) has further developed this work. He found that patients asked inappropriate questions and gave inappropriate answers. They also asked significantly more questions overall in normal conversation. He concluded that in his observations of communication in schizophrenia,

> the problem for schizophrenic patients [had] much less [to do with] . . . the cognitive processes of regulating and organising their thoughts than [with] the social processes of expressing and communicating those thoughts in a way which the listener could understand and follow. Where their difficulty really lay was in taking the role of the other.

This provides an excellent theoretical basis for the use of role play, as well as a focus for understanding and then altering communication abnormalities. Rather than assuming that the speech confusion solely reflects underlying confusion, a therapist who takes an educative stance may assist a patient in modifying speech production to make it more understandable. In practice, this means the following:

1. Helping a patient to recognize that what he says may not be understood.
2. Helping the patient to communicate more clearly by putting him in the listener's position, and then using more precise or clearly understandable speech.

3. Checking with the patient that the therapist has been understood.

Using techniques of this type, Satel and Sledge (1989) were successful in using audiotape feedback with two patients to correct language abnormalities. One believed that "her mother had hypnotized her as a child and given her medication that would cause her to be confused about her past" (p. 103). The audiotaped interviews, introduced after a firm rapport had been developed, had a therapeutic effect on her, enhancing her "reality perception through objectification of her own processes" (p. 1013). With the other patient, more specific assistance with communication led to improvement.

NEW WORDS AND METAPHORICAL SPEECH

One specific aspect of schizophrenic language disturbance is the development of new words (neologisms), which will inevitably impair communication. However, such words are often condensations or hybridizations (Scharfetter, 1980; Arieti, 1974). That is, new words are produced by joining old ones together in a way similar to the process by which language is believed to have evolved (Fromkin & Rodman, 1988), and appropriate linguistic rules for word formation are generally followed. For example, the term "decatastrophization," used later in this book, could be described as a neologism; nevertheless, its roots are clear, and it is a term that would not be beyond the understanding of the intelligent layman.

Patients appear to develop neologisms in similar ways. For example, one of our patients (see Part II, Study 13) spoke of "hyperthought" because of a wish to communicate a concept for which there was no word that he (or anyone else, for that matter) knew. In discussion with him, it emerged that he was attempting to describe his belief that there existed a group of superior beings who could think on a higher level than himself and whom he wanted to join, so that he could also "hyperthink." Crucially, however, "decatastrophization" has been accepted by a group of people (cognitive therapists), and so it is no longer a personally developed word with a private meaning that is not shared by others. This was not the case with "hyperthought."

To complicate matters further, it is also possible that a patient whose vocabulary is limited may produce neologisms in cases where there are already accepted words for the concepts he is attempting to describe. This will increase the confused nature of his attempts to communicate. Metaphorical speech (at times quite poetic) can develop, and an understanding of the idiomatic speech of the patient's cultural background may assist the therapist in unraveling it. Given time, as with the neologism discussed above, patients can frequently trace back the meaning of seemingly incomprehensible language (Foudraine, 1971), and possibly accept alternatives that are linguistically accurate. Scharfetter (1980) notes that when "the examiner knows the patient well, he can sometimes make sense out of the confusion" (p. 118).

NONVERBAL COMMUNICATION

Nonverbal communication in schizophrenia has also been shown to be abnormal in a large number of studies. For example, Walker and colleagues (1984) demonstrated that although people with schizophrenia are capable of deciphering facial cues of identity, they are impaired in their ability to extract salient emotional cues from faces. Walker et al. observed: "The failure to accurately read non-verbal cues of emotion may contribute to inappropriate social responses, as well as decreasing the patient's sense of social efficacy" (p. 43).

Cramer and colleagues (1989) used audiovisual tapes of emotional situations (developed for training raters of levels of "expressed emotion"). These were shown to patients and controls, who were then asked to rate the emotional level of the scenes against an adjective checklist. The patients with schizophrenia failed to detect the dominant character of the scenes, and often perceived the opposite emotions to those perceived by the controls. Such deviant responses were not related to paranoid symptoms, flattened affect, formal thought disorder, general level of morbidity, or duration of inpatient stay. Cramer et al. reviewed further studies examining the judgment of emotional states of others by people with schizophrenia, using photographs and audiotape recordings; these uniformly demonstrated a marked discrepancy between those with schizophrenia and controls.

One of the early psychological theories of the development of schizophrenia, the double-bind theory of Bateson et al. (1956), essentially suggested that confusion might be caused by discrepancies between what a parent said (i.e., verbal expression) and what the parent actually did or intended (i.e., nonverbal communication). However, Williams (1974) in experimental analysis in schizophrenia, found that people with schizophrenia were not upset by conflicting verbal–nonverbal signals. They were simply much less responsive generally than were controls to nonverbal communication. This is therefore not directly supportive of the theory, although it does not, of course, disprove it for specific individuals. The absence of response may be a way of adapting to confusing signals by reducing the anxiety that such a situation would engender.

One would anticipate that social skills training could improve nonverbal communication and increase subjective feelings of comfort. Although the former particularly has been demonstrated, generalization outside the training environment has been more difficult to show, with only limited effects on clinical symptoms and in dealing with real-life problems.

Although understanding of and training in social skills may be of benefit in improving communication and relationship formation, it is possible that it may also be of benefit to patients with thought interference or alienation. Through a lack of knowledge of the very existence of nonverbal communication, some patients appear to misinterpret sensitive perceptions by others of how they are feeling or what they are wanting to do. They may develop beliefs from this that staff members, relatives, or other patients can read or interfere with their thoughts, possibly by some telepathic process. Following on from that, they may fear that thoughts can be taken out of their minds (particularly in cases where they are blocking thoughts in the presence of others) or inserted (in cases where thoughts, perhaps sexual or aggressive, are arising that distress them or are perceived as ego-alien—"I could never think something as revolting or disgusting as that"). Experimental evidence to support such suppositions, however, is presently lacking.

CONCLUSIONS

Being unable to communicate clearly is a major handicap in an already confusing condition. Although it is true that if thoughts are confused, communication will also be confused, it may nevertheless be possible to improve communication by assisting patients when it is failing, then having them "take the role of the other," and checking that the resulting communication is understood. Neologisms and metaphorical speech can be discussed and alternatives suggested. Finally education in nonverbal communication may be useful, possibly in combating misunderstandings arising from the lack of knowledge about it.

Identity

BREAKDOWN IN EGO BOUNDARIES

Many authors describe a fundamental deficit in schizophrenia as a breakdown of personal boundaries, or, more specifically, ego boundaries. Fischman (1983) reviews such work in his description of dreams, hallucinogenic drug states, and schizophrenia, and concludes that

> in these states, the ego's capacity to average or synthesize various self-representations into a continuous, coherent self is compromised—leading to an impairment of the reality-orientated secondary [that is, reasoning and logical] process, and the emergence of the florid attributes of the primary [that is, more primitive, drive-related] process. (p. 73)

He describes Federn (1952) as using

> the term "ego boundaries" to denote a dynamic set of temporo-spatial limits which divide experience into past, present, and future; internal and external; real and unreal . . . the ego [presents] a unique paradox because it is normally experienced as both subject and object at once. . . . in incipient psychosis or, in healthy persons, upon falling asleep, the ego (self-representation) boundaries lose their cathexis . . . accurate perception of reality depends on the ego's continuous averaging of self-representations to form a constant frame of reference. (pp. 77–78)

Certainly the complex and potentially fragile process by which differentiation between what is external and internal occurs is flawed in schizophrenia. Hallucinations arise because thoughts originating from within come to sound like voices or appear as visions (and likewise for other sensory modalities) from without. Control of one's own internal thoughts, feelings, or actions may come to appear to be controlled or influenced by external forces.

Furthermore, as Freeman and colleagues (1958) commented in their investigation of patients with chronic schizophrenia, "the most direct result of the breakdown of ego boundaries is the schizophrenic patient's confusion regarding his own identity. All . . . [our] patients, at one time or another gave evidence that they were unsure of their personal identity" (p. 52). As a result, patients may have difficulty distinguishing between themselves and others. Freeman et al., noted that institutional practices such as "pooled" clothing systems in mental hospitals and the size of wards in the not-so-distant past (such as one they described consisting of 70 patients) exacerbated this confusion. Individualized care thus has definite theoretical justification, as well as seeming to be humane and grounded in common sense. It appears even more important than is normally the case to assist those with schizophrenia to define their individual identities. The implicit assumption justifying grouping practices in, for example, large institutions—that such practices make little difference to the patients—is increasingly recognized as extremely misguided and a major contributor to the disabilities originally deemed part of the underlying illness.

Frequently patients discuss this uncertainty about who they are—"Why are we here?" or "What is the meaning of our existence?"—in ways that are characteristic of adolescence. Erikson (1965) describes the adolescent period as one of the resolution of "identity versus role confusion" (p. 252) in the growth of the ego. He describes how "all sameness and continuities relied on earlier are more or less questioned again" (p. 252) and also elaborates on the importance at this stage of social contacts in resolution of these conflicts. Such questioning can in itself be stressful and is inevitably inconclusive, although sources ranging from philosophical and religious treatises, through more accessible works such as Frankl's

(1959) *Man's Search for Meaning*, to Charles Schulz's *Peanuts* cartoons, can be used to provide some acceptable compromises. Erikson also discusses the possible "role confusion" over sexual identity and the inability to settle on an occupational identity as related to "outright psychotic episodes" (p. 253).

Certainly these issues are ones frequently encountered in patients with schizophrenia; and although they are commoner in cases with earlier onset, they may be encountered as unresolved issues in those presenting later in life. Accepting their importance to each patient and allowing him to discuss such concerns can be a profitable way of establishing and sustaining rapport and of developing rational thinking strategies.

DIFFERENTIATING FROM PARENTS

The differentiation of one's own identity from that of one's parents is a necessary task that may be more difficult in a person with schizophrenia, who, perhaps because of perceptual and attentional deficits (Brenner, 1989), finds the boundary between himself and others indistinct. This will be a factor in family situations and may lead to more fraught and frantic attempts to create such a division (see Figure 7.1). Although parents may attempt to frustrate these efforts by overprotec-

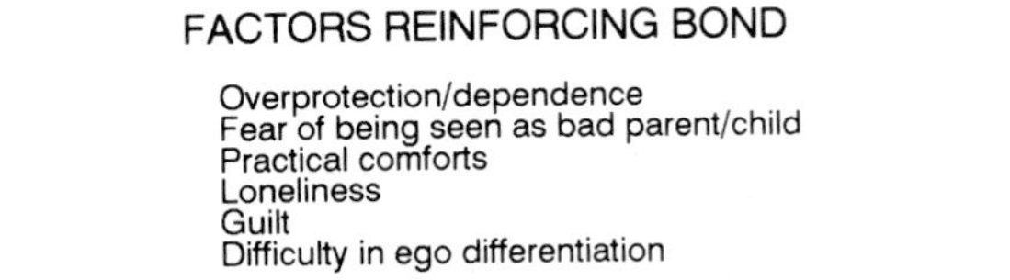

Normal parent-child separation
Need for ego differentiation
Hostility
Criticism

FACTORS BREAKING DOWN BOND

PARENT _____ PATIENT

FACTORS REINFORCING BOND

Overprotection/dependence
Fear of being seen as bad parent/child
Practical comforts
Loneliness
Guilt
Difficulty in ego differentiation

FIGURE 7.1. Some factors complicating parent–patient relationship in schizophrenia.

tive strategies, the evidence for this is limited. That they may act in a confused and confusing way in their concern, and perhaps also out of feelings of guilt about the patient and themselves, is not only understandable but concurs with evidence that a proportion of parents (Boker et al., 1989) have similar problems with their own identity boundaries.

The studies on the place of critical expressed emotion and the influence of "face-to-face" contact as a factor in relapse (Leff & Vaughn, 1980) are also of clear relevance to this. Unfortunately, criticism of families (albeit increasingly covert) by mental health professionals, exemplified by such statements as that in schizophrenia "the victims . . . do not just go mad, but are driven mad—and driven there characteristically by their parents" (Hudson, 1975) increase guilt and confusion and creates distress rather than alleviating it. Such criticism requires modification at least as much as criticism of patients by families does. Attempts to reinforce identity and ego boundaries through reality testing therefore have a rational basis to them. The discussion of hallucinations in the next chapter illustrates this further.

CONCLUSIONS

Difficulties in developing and sustaining personal identity— "where I stop and the rest of the world begins"—are frequent if not to a degree universal in schizophrenia. This is particularly important in relation to other family members, who, as experimental evidence suggests, may have similar difficulties. There needs to be an awareness that this may lead to compensatory "marking out of territory" by the apparent use of hostile or critical expression. Philosophical questions may arise and need to be dealt with sensitively. Individualization of care is essential.

Hallucinations

DEFINING HALLUCINATIONS

In 1572, Lavater first used the term "hallucinate" to refer to "ghostes and spirites walking by nyght"; the Greek and Latin derivation is from "to wander in mind." Asaad and Shapiro (1986) describe how the term then came to describe behavior that is intended as serious by the person engaging in it, but is perceived as heedless and foolish by an observer. Esquirol's 1837 description became the basis for the current definition of a hallucination as the "apparent perception of an external object where no such object is present" (Critchley & Rossall, 1978, p. 64). The marked similarity of dreams to hallucinations has been noted by many observers (e.g., Slade, 1976), including Freud.

Hallucinations are not uncommon. The Epidemiologic Catchment Survey in the United States sought to investigate this by asking, "Have you ever had the experience of seeing something or someone that others who are present could not see—that is, had a vision when you were completely awake?", and similar questions for other sense modalities. No fewer than 10–15% of the population reported experiencing hallucinations, with an annual incidence (rate of occurrence) of 4–5% (Tien, 1992). This finding has been given support by Romme et al. (1992), who have described examples of large numbers of people who reported hearing voices but were not troubled by them.

In their wide-ranging review of experimental evidence and theories about hallucinations, Asaad and Shapiro (1986) conclude that "all people either do hallucinate (in waking states, in dreams, as part of psychiatric disorders) or can be made to hallucinate with a variety of drugs (hallucinogens) or states of deprivation" (p. 1094). By contrast, Slade (1976) reported that hallucinations could not be produced by direct electrical stimulation of the brain in more than a relatively small (7.7%) group of epileptic patients with whom such experiments were performed. However, under conditions of sensory deprivation, up to 50% of volunteers had visual and auditory experiences. Whether Asaad and Shapiro's broadening of the conventional definition of "hallucination" is warranted or not, it would certainly seem that hallucinations are far more common than is generally recognized.

Critchley and Rossall (1978) have compared the concept of a hallucination with that of an illusion, which is "the distortion (or transposition) of perceptive data," and imagery, which is "an experience that receives or copies a previous perceptual experience in the absence of the original sensory stimulation" (p. 64). They note that

> selected and unselected stimuli have a collective function in maintaining the normal waking organisation of brain function. . . . Accidents and errors by long-distance night truck drivers (highway hypnosis), jet pilots, and radar sentinels become more understandable when it is realised that they are caused by the perceptual distortions and impaired concentration that result from altered sensory stimulation. (p. 64)

Three essential criteria for hallucinations have been defined (Slade, 1976):

1. A hallucination is a "percept-like experience" that occurs in the absence of an external stimulus.
2. A hallucination is a "percept-like experience" that has the full force and impact of a real perception (Aggernaes, 1972). Thus it does not seem to be in "inner subjective space"— that is, "in one's mind." In other words, a "voice" sounds the same as if a person was speaking directly; a "vision" is like something seen in the normal way; and so on. A hallucination may, however, vary in intensity, and a clear demarcation from

obsessional ideas may at times prove difficult. Obsessional ideas are repetitive thoughts that the person wishes to be rid of but that he recognizes as originating in his own mind.

3. A hallucination is a "percept-like experience" that is unwilled, occurs spontaneously, and cannot be readily controlled by the percipient. This distinguishes it from memory and imagination.

FACTORS CAUSING OR EXACERBATING HALLUCINATIONS

In discussing causes or etiology, Asaad and Shapiro (1986) suggest that

> any integrative theory of hallucinations must postulate the failure of a screening mechanism which functions during waking and most non-Rapid Eye Movement sleep stages and is "turned off" during REM sleep. Furthermore, it would seem that the nature of this "on–off switch," or screening mechanism, lies at the heart of the biological component of hallucinations. (p. 1094)

They suggest that in psychosis a neurotransmitter-mediated or receptor dysfunction (a vulnerability factor) permits the failure of this normal inhibitory mechanism and thus the emergence of the symptom of hallucination during the waking state, equivalent to "dreaming awake." "Dreaming awake" is a term that many patients find quite descriptive of their experiences and that can be reassuring and destigmatizing.

One might anticipate that those who develop hallucinations would show differences in imagery—that is, would have more vivid imaginations than those who do not hallucinate. However, Chandiramani and Varma (1987) have been unable to demonstrate such differences in patients with schizophrenia compared with normal controls. They have noted that the literature is generally inconclusive.

It is well recognized nonetheless that emotionally charged events—for example, road traffic accidents—produce more vivid imagery that is "etched into the mind" (similarly drug "flashbacks" and even catchy tunes). It is possible that the intense anxiety that so frequently accompanies the onset of hallucinations may be a factor in their recurrence and persistence. The meaning invested in hallucinations may also be of importance—whether a person says to himself, "The devil is talking to me" or "I must be going crazy," or, dismissively; "That was a strange sensation, I must have been overtired." Emotional significance may reinforce auditory and visual imagery, as in post-traumatic stress disorder (Wilcox et al., 1991), and may be of relevance. Persistence of hallucinations has been demonstrated by Judkins and Slade (1981) to be related to hostility. The early reduction of hostility, anxiety, and distress may therefore be of considerable importance.

Allen and Agus (1968) have described how hyperventilation can lead to a precipitation of hallucinations. They provide two detailed case studies, obtained while they were working on the medical staff of a penal institution:

1. A "borderline subnormal," schizoid 17-year-old admitted to the institution became distressed and started hallucinating (however, diagnostic signs of schizophrenia are not given in the case study). Hyperventilation was demonstrated to bring on the hallucinations experimentally on a number of occasions.

2. A 17-year-old of average intelligence was diagnosed as having a "schizophrenic reaction" prior to being committed to the institution. Hyperventilation produced visual and auditory hallucinations.

Allen and Agus note that in various primitive cultures a medicine man raising a group to a pitch of frenzy can activate anxiety and fear as well as ecstasy; the anxiety induces hyperventilation, which gradually builds up, leading to the changes described. They cite evidence that in some Native American tribes a combination of starvation and torture was used to induce hallucinations. It would therefore seem reasonable to see what effect anxiety management and relaxation techniques may have on hallucinations.

Slade (1973) describes in detail the hallucinatory experiences of a patient who completed multiple records of mood state, environmental variables, and the hearing of voices. He was found to be more likely to hear voices when in a state of relatively high internal arousal in a noisy, crowded situation in which he was not engaged in conversation. Training in Jacobson's muscle relaxation technique, together with desensitization using the patient's imagining of how he would feel in the situation described above, was used initially, but no change in the voices resulted. The patient was noted to have difficulty in recognizing and reporting changes in his anxiety level, which possibly impaired imaginal desensitization. *In vivo* ("real-life") desensitization, however, had a marked effect; the focus was on exposure to more people, to whom the patient was encouraged to talk by therapists.

Suggestibility may also be of importance. A potential source of misinterpretation may be "phosphenes"—sparks of light produced by pressure, sudden movement, and traction on the globe of the eye. In organic hallucinosis, the quality of mental imagery and psychodynamic factors have been noted

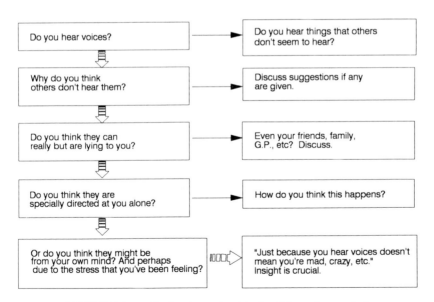

FIGURE 8.1. Hallucinations: A critical collaborative analysis.

(Critchley & Rossall, 1978) to influence the content of hallu-cinations. Critchley and Rossall observe that

> entoptic visions [that is, associated with blindness, . . . are made up of] a series of simple elements and argued that the images from anatomical structures such as the retinal ganglionic network and from "luminous dust" which are normally filtered out from conscious perception impinge upon the deranged mind and are misconstrued [as these visions]. (p. 85)

This could also be occurring with phosphenes: They may act as the substrate for misinterpretation under circumstances in which the patient is markedly suggestible.

Bentall and Slade (1985) summarize further evidence for suggestibility effects in an investigation of reality-testing deficiencies that may occur in hallucinators. Using a reality-testing analysis based on "signal detection theory," the investigators matched patients who hallucinated with control patients and found that the former were significantly more likely to detect a "signal" when one was not present.

Sedman (1966b) discusses the experience of thoughts being apparently audible. He notes that various forms of auditory imagery described by patients—"inner voices," "loud" or "audible thoughts," and even the "voice of conscience"—are often experienced in an obsessive–compulsive way that closely resembles the schizophrenic experience. At times this "shaded over into various forms of 'thought echoing' " (p. 485). The distinction he makes between "inner voices" as obsessive–compulsive phenomena and a "hallucination proper" is that the latter "is alien to the person's experience" (p. 490). It is therefore the attribution of the experienced phenomena that is crucial, rather than the phenomena themselves.

CONCLUSIONS

Hallucinations are remarkably common. Evidence suggests that emotional trauma, sleep disturbance, and suggestibility may be significant in their generation and perpetuation. Providing assistance in reality testing (see Figure 8.1 and Part II) and in recognition of anxiety, and then providing anxiety management training (including exposure to feared situations), would therefore seem reasonable strategies with hallucinating patients.

Coping Strategies

Increasingly over the past decade, consideration has been given to the possibility that patients may not be impotent in relation to their symptoms; they may be able to exercise control over them, or at least may develop an ability to cope with them. This idea is not new. Jaspers (1913/1963) reported that patients could counter certain psychotic phenomena by distraction or some effort of will. Arieti (1974) described a "listening attitude" toward "voices" and a "referential attitude" toward delusions of reference (e.g., the idea that people on television are referring to a patient), both of which he believed patients could modify.

However, psychiatric texts have not made much mention of this possibility. Hamilton (1984) suggests only that patients should be advised to ignore their "voices" and delusions. The implication is that psychosocial management of acute psychotic symptoms is at best peripheral, and that medication is our only effective tool in direct modification of such symptoms.

RESEARCH ASSESSING PATIENTS' COPING STRATEGIES

In 1981, Falloon and Talbot investigated 40 patients with persistent auditory hallucinations and uncovered three groups of strategies they used to cope with these symptoms:

1. *Behavior change* (e.g., change in posture and in inter-

personal contact). Many of the patients did not initially relate such behavior change to an attempt to cope with hallucinations, because it had become habitual. Most described speaking with people as helping generally.

2. *Efforts to lower physiological arousal* (i.e., use of methods of relaxation, such as listening to soothing music to reduce symptoms).

3. *Cognitive coping methods.* Patients made attempts at attentional control by trying to divert their attention, or at suppression of hallucinations by trying to ignore them. Attitudinal change was another method used; the patients might listen attentively to the voices and often accepted their guidance to reduce the distress associated with resistance. The explanation that hallucinations are similar to dreams experienced when wide awake was noted. Falloon and Talbot found that generally males and females used similar techniques. Their "non-depressed" group showed more acceptance of the "voices" and appeared more reconciled to their persistence.

Tarrier (1987), replicating this work, studied 25 patients of whom three-quarters specified coping strategies. In turn, three-quarters of these reported at least one of these strategies as being at least moderately successful.

Carr (1988) looked in detail at 200 patients with schizophrenia who demonstrated a total of 310 coping responses. These were grouped, fairly similarly to Falloon and Talbot's (1981), as follows:

1. *Behavior control.* This was used by 83%; 38% applied it to delusions, and 43% to hallucinations. Five subgroups emerged:

a. *"Distraction" involving passive diversion* (e.g., listening to the radio, listening to music, watching TV) *or active diversion* (e.g., playing a musical instrument, writing a diary, writing poetry, reading, or gardening). Collins and colleagues (1989) described the experiences of one patient in using different types of modified auditory input through headphones to cope with and decrease the occurrence of hallucinations. They found significant improvements with tapes of interesting speech and music.

b. *Physical change involving body movement.* Inactivity or passivity (i.e., rest, relaxation, or sleep) was especially frequently used with thinking disturbance. Alternatively, activity (e.g., walking, running, or swimming) or postural change was used; this seemed to be a way of changing a state of mind, summoning up resources, and resuming a state of composure.

c. *Indulgence* (e.g., eating, smoking, or drinking).

d. *Nonspecific techniques* (e.g., "I keep myself busy," "I try to do something enjoyable").

2. *Socialization.* This was very frequently used and included talking to family or friends. Perhaps surprisingly, social avoidance or withdrawal as a conscious coping method was hardly ever reported. (This was also noted by Tarrier, 1987.)

3. *Cognitive control.* Three subgroups emerged:

a. *Suppression of unwanted thoughts or perceptions* ("I try not to think about it," "I ignore them").

b. *Shifted attention* (redirection of attention toward neutral, comforting, or less distracting ideas).

c. *Problem solving*—specifically, focusing on resolving some difficulty or planning a future task ("I think about setting up projects," "I concentrate on being a better person").

4. *Medical care.* Carr described this as relatively rare; it included using or changing medication, going to a hospital, or going to see a mental health worker.

5. *Symptomatic behaviors.* Carr noted that the intention of these was to relieve discomfort, but that they resulted in expression of illness-related behavior. Examples included contacting the police for protection, acting in an angry or aggressive way, shouting demands to be left alone, or telling the voices to "shut up." Patients might, however, act on delusional ideas for subjective relief while being aware of their deviant or bizarre nature.

Carr (1988) has suggested that the link among these diverse strategies may be that they all relate to the phenomenon of attention. At present, patients use coping techniques such as these in isolation and almost surreptitiously. Tarrier (1987) has suggested that given the benefit ascribed to them by patients, we should not only be encouraging their use, but educating and training patients in finding out and using which-ever techniques they individually find useful. Recently Tarrier and colleagues (1993) have taken this next logical step—capitalizing on the coping strategies patients already employ by teaching them to build on these skills, in a self-management procedure named "coping strategy enhancement."

Cohen and Berk (1985), in a study of 86 patients, at-tempted to assess which broad coping styles (as opposed to specific strategies) were used for which symptoms. They found that the following styles were used for the following problems:

1. "Fighting back" in dealing with depression, psychotic symptoms, interpersonal problems, and drug/alcohol abuse.
2. "Time out" and "social diversion" for anxiety.
3. "Medical strategies" for anxiety and schizophrenic symptoms.
4. "Feelings of helplessness" for schizophrenic and inter-personal problems.
5. "Acceptance of symptoms" for depression, interper-sonal problems, and drug/alcohol abuse.
6. "Prayer" exclusively for schizophrenic thoughts.

The least used of these were social diversion and prayer.

Nelson et al. (1991) studied 20 patients with schizophren-ia who had persistent auditory hallucinations, and examined the use of earplugs, subvocal counting (e.g., "1, 2, 3, 1, 2, 3, . . ." under a patient's breath), and use of a portable cassette recorder to listen to music. The last of these was most popular and effective, followed by use of the earplugs, with some also finding benefit from counting. Nelson et al. have suggested that these methods may work by shifting attention and redu-cing anxiety. Their use as adjuncts to pharmacological treat-ments has been commended, because of their noninvasive nature and lack of side effects. Previous studies have demon-strated that the ear in which an earplug is placed (i.e., whether it affects the dominant or nondominant hemisphere) is not related to efficacy.

PATIENTS' DESCRIPTIONS OF
COPING STRATEGIES

A further way of exploring coping strategies is to examine patients' own descriptions of their illness. Hatfield (1989) in her review of these, states that patients, rather than being "withdrawn and passive . . . are actively fighting 'internal terrors and external realities' to keep their emotional balance and social composure in a world they cannot always translate" (p. 1143). One patient described by Hatfield dealt with the "unfairness of having mental illness by accepting the fact that life is not fair, although it is unfair in different ways to different people" (p. 1144). Hatfield also mentions joining a self-help group, an example of which would be the "voices" group established by the National Schizophrenia Fellowship in Great Britain.

Romme and Escher (1989), as noted in Chapter 1, have recently described a community sample's experiences. After Romme went on a TV program with one of their patients to describe a coping strategy for hallucinations, 450 people who heard voices made contact. Of these, 150 felt they could "handle" their voices; 300 could not. At a congress attended by 300 people who heard voices, 20 of these patients were selected to talk about how they coped. The following phases were described by the patients as relevant to coping with voices:

1. The "startling" phase; usually the voices were sudden in onset, and were primarily perceived at first as frightening experiences.
2. The "organization" phase, or the process of selection and communication with the voices.
3. The "stabilization phase," or the period in which a more consistent way of handling the voices was acquired.

During the startling phase, one patient described the following in learning to cope:

1. Fear, anxiety, and a desire to escape.

2. Investigating what the voices meant and accepting the voices as "independent beings" [*sic*].

3. Accepting herself, exploring what she was trying to escape from, reversing the confrontation with the voices, and not trying to escape any more.

Of Romme and Escher's original 450 respondents, 70% described the voices as beginning after some traumatic (emotional) event—an accident (4%); divorce or death (14%); a psychotherapy session (12%); a spiritualist session, for example, with a medium (4%); or other events, such as illness, being in love, moving, or pregnancy (36%). Those who heard voices after a trauma described two general impacts. Some described them as helpful, viewed them positively, and considered them part of the internal self; others were negative from the beginning and did not generally view the voices as parts of the self or as internally generated phenomena.

During the phase of organization, many patients became confused and wished to escape. Initial panic and a feeling of powerlessness were followed by a period of anger against the voices. The latter did not seem fruitful as a coping strategy. Ignoring them was frequently attempted, but only 33% of the patients were able to do so successfully. The effort spent on trying to ignore the voices often led to a curtailment in the scope of their activities. The "most fruitful strategies" were to select positive voices and listen and talk only to them, trying to understand them. Accepting voices seemed important as part of a "process of growth toward taking responsibility for one's own decisions." "Drawing limits" or "structuring the contract," with or without repetitive acts, was also a technique used (Romme & Escher, 1989, p. 212).

During the phase of stabilization, the patients came to see their voices as part of themselves. They could choose between following the advice of the voices or their own ideas. A great many frames of reference were used by those hearing voices—psychodynamic, mystical, parapsychological, and medical. These have been described in some detail in Chapter 1.

Miller and colleagues (1993) have looked further at "patients' attitudes to hallucinations" (p. 584). They identified nine qualities viewed positively and negatively and illustrated them with comments from their subjects. Positive effects were reported by 52%:

1. Relaxing, soothing: "In a way, if I can keep it low, it's relaxing, like having a radio on."
2. Companionship: "Recently I'd ask all the time to hear it. I was lonely; I wanted some friends."
3. Financial: "It made it easier because my mother put me on SSI (Supplementary Security Income)."
4. Defensive, protective: "I hallucinated shooting my dad instead of actually shooting him. . . . If my father was getting ready to do something to me, they'd wake me up."
5. Self-concept: "It has made me feel more attractive. . . ."
6. Reactions of others: "I thought people would be nicer to me because I had a handicap. . . ."
7. Performance: "I need to hear the voices, to maintain well-being—by picking up my room, or getting something to eat, when they tell me to."
8. Relationships: "The voices make it easier for me to be close to people."
9. Sexual: "My sexual desire has increased recently, due to the love of the man that I feel I know via hallucinations. . . ." (pp. 586–587)

In contrast, adverse effects were commented on by 94%:

1. Financial: "I'll never be able to get a job because of this."
2. Emotional distress, tension: "There is no peace and quiet unless I am in a deep sleep."
3. Performance: ". . . the voices get in the way of my work. . . ."
4. Reactions of others: "I feel they think I'm crazy . . . It scares them to death."
5. Feeling endangered or threatened: "Sometimes the voices say they're going to kill me. . . ."

6. Relationships: "I might have a friend I go visit. They'll tell me stories about what he does ... it can impact on the friendship"
7. Self-concept: "The visions ... look so handsome. ... I'm uglier."
8. Loneliness: "They don't keep you company."
9. Sexual: "It got in the way of sex; I feel like I'm on TV." (p. 587)

Miller and colleagues concluded that "a sizeable number ... believe that their hallucinations have adaptive as well as maladaptive functions" (p. 588) but nevertheless only 12% unambiguously wished to continue hallucinating. Their work provides valuable insights into the effects and possible functions of hallucinations. Where these are maladaptive, the hallucinations may act as a signpost to areas of dysfunction or difficulty such that coping strategies could be targeted on the specific functions that the hallucinations appear to have. For example, if they are considered soothing, develop relaxation methods; if they have relationship functions, explore other avenues for developing relationships such as self-help or particular interest groups; if sexual functions, assess whether sexual dysfunction or experience of sexual abuse is a factor; if threatening, clarify the status of hallucinations as voices or visions which in themselves are powerless, but also explore any threats, perceived or actual, in the person's environment.

PATIENTS' VERSUS RELATIVES' COPING STRATEGIES

Boker, Brenner, and colleagues (Boker et al., 1989; Brenner et al., 1987) have taken a quite different approach to the investigation of coping ("autoprotective") strategies: They have compared patients with their relatives and to normal controls, in order to determine whether any differences emerge among these groups. They have shown that patients with schizophrenia have difficulties in processing information compared to normal controls. Using psychological tests, they have also demonstrated that some relatives show these difficulties.

When Brenner, Boker, and colleagues assessed coping strategies in these groups, they found that unaffected relatives interpreted unpleasant feelings, concentration difficulties, and the like in the same way as normal controls—that is, by using everyday explanatory models, such as fatigue, lack of interest, or insecurity at work. They were not troubled by these occurrences; as a result, their compensatory efforts mainly included taking a break, engaging in strengthening exercises, and switching to other activities. Other relatives and people with schizophrenia experienced these problems as varying signs of oncoming deterioration in their state of health. The main aim of their coping behavior was to reduce tension.

In problem-solving-oriented coping attempts, however, relatives and people with schizophrenia differed. Patients preferred coping attempts directly oriented to behavior, whose main purpose seemed to be in soothing anxiety. Affected relatives attempted conscious mental confrontations with the problems, leading to long-lasting re-evaluation of the situation. Both patients and affected relatives had a significantly more external locus of control than did nonaffected relatives; that is, they felt less in control themselves and more under the control of others or external forces. Patients considered their internal control ability to be determined by their efforts significantly more than by their skills, compared to both groups of relatives. Patients reported significantly more "emotional involvement" and a tendency to "give up" in situations of stress, and more "expectation of help by others and need of social support" than relatives. Overall, there seem to be a number of different ways in which patients' coping strategies differ from those of normal controls and the different groups of relatives; these seem very relevant in developing treatment strategies.

Focusing more specifically on relatives' coping responses, Birchwood and Cochrane (1990), in a study of 53 relatives of patients with schizophrenia, identified eight categories of coping behavior used:

1. Constructive—noncoercive actions taken to ameliorate behaviors.
2. Ignoring/accepting—actions involving a benign acceptance of or indifference to nonproblematic behavior.
3. Resigned—actions similar to the preceding, but following initial unsuccessful efforts to produce change.
4. Avoidant—actions designed to minimize relatives' exposure to the individual's behavior.
5. Reassuring—actions specifically centered on symptoms, in which relatives presented a stable and calm exterior, emphasizing the security of their home and their relationship.
6. Coercive—punitive or critical actions that might involve verbal or physical aggression, threats, attempts to shame or embarrass the patient, or attempt to confront the patient in other ways.
7. Collusive—actions that might involve actively condoning or supporting symptomatic behavior.
8. Disorganized—inconsistent actions expressing desperation and helplessness.

In the few families reporting the presence of aggression (5%), submission, conflict, and avoidance strategies were used. It was recognized that these styles of coping were used with a considerable degree of consistency across a range of situations, independently of prevailing behavioral disturbance with two important exceptions to this: Some relatives were more likely to become disorganized with increasing level of disturbance, whereas others were more likely to use reassurance. And lastly, but of considerable importance, coercion was a more probable strategy in cases where the patients showed greater withdrawal and inactivity, and also in those with a greater number of relapses/readmissions.

CONCLUSIONS

Rather than passively accepting their symptoms, most patients and relatives seem to have evolved or worked out for themselves some useful strategies to reduce the distress the patients' symptoms can cause. These widely varied strategies include changing behavior patterns, increasing social interactions, distraction and other methods of cognitive control. Cohen and Berk (1985) in their investigation, noted that "during the course of the interviews we were struck by the patients' surprise and pleasure that anyone would devote substantial time to examining the methods that they had devised for managing their symptoms" (p. 409). It does seem remarkable that until recently so little attention has been given to such an important area.

Negative Symptoms

Although the "positive symptoms" described up to this point can have seriously disrupting consequences, can be extremely distressing to patient and families, and are not infrequently resistant to pharmacological treatments, therapists seem much more optimistic about managing them than about managing the "negative symptoms." Low motivation, low drive, withdrawal, and perceived lack of response to medication seem to constitute an affront to our therapeutic zeal. But perhaps this very frustration—as well as that of the patients' friends and relatives, and more still that of the patients themselves—is a major factor in the production, maintenance, and expression of this negativity.

FACTORS CAUSING AND MAINTAINING NEGATIVE SYMPTOMS

Strauss and colleagues (1989) state that "it is crucial to explore possible psychological and social factors in negative symptoms in order to understand the symptoms more fully and to provide a basis for more adequate prevention and treatment" (p. 128). They suggest two hypotheses regarding these symptoms. The first hypothesis is that "negative symptoms arise in many instances as responses to extremely difficult psychological and social situations. These symptoms may even help the person with schizophrenia to survive" (p. 128). Strauss et al. describe in detail the sources of the stress patients experience:

1. Psychological contributors.
    a. The pain of relapse into positive symptoms. (Positive

symptoms are distressing and psychologically painful in themselves; the fear of lapsing into them may
in itself be stressful.)
  b. The loss of hope and self-esteem.
  c. The possibility of impulsive or bizarre behavior.
  d. Problems in finding a new identity as a "nonpatient."
  e. The feeling of guilt for past dysfunction.
  f. The potential threat of entering complex, stressful
     social situations.
  g. Situations where the person is rendered helpless by
     the disorder, by environmental features, or both.
2. Environmental contributors.
  a. Institutionalization.
  b. The social benefit system.
  c. The stigma of schizophrenia.

Strauss et al.'s (1989) second hypothesis is that "negative
symptoms have a psychological and social impact on the further course of the disorder" (p. 128). The authors state:

> These symptoms generate positive feedback mechanisms
> that maintain or exacerbate the disorder with its dysfunc-
> tion. . . . patients who are too withdrawn [and] apathetic
> . . . cut themselves off from the very sources that provide
> motivation, structure, hope, material assistance, and ad-
> vice. . . . the diagnosis of schizophrenia is almost unique
> amongst mental disorders in terms of the despair it
> evokes. (pp. 130–131)

As described in Chapter 9, Hatfield (1989) has looked at
patients' accounts of schizophrenia. She identifies several
sources of stress in patients' accounts:

1. *Altered perceptions—increasing acuteness or enhancement.*
Things seemed brighter to patients, sounded louder, and
changed unpredictably. A sense of coherence, described by
Hatfield as "an enduring though dynamic feeling of confidence that one's internal and external environments are pred-
ictable and that things will work out as well as can be expected"
(p. 1142), is suggested as crucial to well-being. This lack plag-

ues the lives of those with schizophrenia. Maintaining a stable world may mean maintaining a relatively unchanging one, manifest in "negative behavior."

2. *Cognitive confusion.* Patients described themselves as "confused," "hazy," "bewildered," and "disoriented." Their sense of time frequently seemed disturbed.

3. *Attentional deficit.* Hatfield describes patients as "captured by a stimulus rather than being able to choose what to attend to." She continues, "finding themselves riveted to a particular stimulus, people with schizophrenia conclude that what they are attracted to has unusual significance" (p. 1143).

4. *Impaired identity.* Patients especially referred to great difficulty in deciding how to characterize what was wrong with them.

Also as noted in Chapter 9, Boker et al. (1989) noted the occurrence of psychotic miniepisodes and asked how patients might be averting relapse. They demonstrated that reaction time and span of concentration were deficient in patients with schizophrenia compared to normal controls. The patients with schizophrenia, however, did not react to subjectively perceived "basic disorders" (unpleasant sensations or perceived inabilities—e.g., to concentrate) solely with avoidance or withdrawal, as might be expected. They were practically unanimous in their interpretation of these basic disorders as "danger signals"; patients with neuroses however, interpreted them as signs of their neurosis. As described in Chapter 9, healthy controls experienced basic disorders totally in terms of everyday psychological explanatory models and were hardly worried by them; consequently, the healthy individuals coped with such disorders mainly by taking a break, trying to regain strength, or the like. Avoidance reactions predominated.

In other words, Boker et al. have made the very important finding for the consideration of negative symptoms that neurotic and healthy individuals experience basic disorders with far less emotional tension and ego-threatening anxiety. Whereas a healthy individual who experiences comparable disturbances will often pause, rest, or switch to another activity, many people with schizophrenia seem stubbornly determined to overcome their deficits. Essentially, they try too hard, and they are often encouraged or even coerced (Birchwood & Cochrane, 1990) in this by their families, friends, and therapists—in all good faith.

Strauss (1989) describes a number of patterns and sequences of schizophrenic illness. He describes one pattern of considerable relevance to consideration of negative symptoms as "woodshedding" (named after a tradition among jazz musicians of retiring to the woodshed to practice before emerging to perform), in which a long plateau in functioning is followed by sudden change.

> This plateau may be characterised, especially after hospital discharge . . . by apathy and withdrawal. Frequently . . . the patient begins to wonder if he will ever get well, the family become increasingly worried, and the clinician wonders if the patient is burning out. . . . Patients then begin to improve and may reach a higher level than they have ever previously accomplished. . . . it appears that the patients are becoming used to the community again, talking with people a little more, gathering their self confidence and recovering a familiarity with non-psychotic life.

One patient described this phenomenon to Strauss as a "long rest in a protected environment" (p. 23). It seems to protect against a relapse into positive symptoms and to allow a healing process to occur. Providing time for healing and a reduction of pressure may allow this to happen. Potentially, maintaining pressure may impede it and protract the negative phase.

MacCarthy and colleagues (1986) looked at task motivation and problem appraisal in long-term psychiatric patients, many of whom had schizophrenia. The patients' assessments of their performance at specific tasks and the major difficulties they encountered were generally in good agreement with those of staff members involved in their care. However, the patients struggled to cope, and some of their coping strategies conflicted with relatives and staff members' attempts (as would be expected from the discussion above)—for example, sleeping in late to assist in coping with auditory hallucinations, and staying up at night because of the quiet and lack of social pressure.

STRATEGIES FOR DEALING WITH NEGATIVE SYMPTOMS

Behavioral psychologists have devised strategies to assist in overcoming negative symptoms (reviewed by Slade & Bentall, 1989). Essentially, these are well-structured programs such as the following:

1. Use of token economies, in which specific rewards are given when desired responses are made; however, positive effects with these appear to be consequences of changes in the way staff members interact with patients rather than of the program itself, which in some ways may be considered demeaning.
2. Social skills training; however, this may have short-term benefits only, and there have been difficulties in generalizing away from the experimental situation.
3. Life skills training.
4. Self-instructional training (Meichenbaum & Cameron, 1973), in which patients learn specific instructions to use in target situations.
5. Problem-solving techniques developed to assist patients in assessing problem situations, devising ways of dealing with them, and then carrying out these solutions and reassessing where failure occurs.

With all these techniques, learning in the experimental situation can be very successful, but generalizing outside them has proved much more difficult. In general terms, it may be that reducing the pressures and expectations that patients impose on themselves and others impose on them can be a more effective means of improving the patients' performance than increasing such pressures.

The technique of paradoxical intention may be useful. This involves setting a target well beneath a patient's capabilities in order to enable him to attain one just within it. For example, one of our patients expressed frustration at being unable to attend a day hospital at a regular time. She aimed to get up at 7 A.M. but only managed this 1 day in 5, on other days she got up between 9 A.M. and 1 P.M. It was suggested that instead she aim to get up late regularly, as "it really doesn't matter too much what time you get into the day hospital." Giving her permission to do this eventually resulted in her regular attendance and ability to rise between 7 and 8 A.M. She has been discharged from the day hospital to attend college, which she is doing regularly—but she has been told that "the most important thing is that you just go along and enjoy it. If you pass any of your exams, that will be a bonus."

Use of structured but realistic activity schedules and programs; considerable amounts of patience; and, perhaps most importantly, the ability to allow the patient to proceed at his own slow pace (or even to stand still for a period of time) would seem the most likely strategies for success.

CONCLUSIONS

Positive approaches to negative symptoms involve understanding how such symptoms may be protective, as Strauss and colleagues describe, and also how they may result from too much rather than too little effort being exercised by family and patient, as Boker and colleagues have demonstrated. Understanding and attempting to resolve confusion, sanctioning avoidance behavior ("to stop banging heads against brick walls"), and structured but very limited activity scheduling (which may include mastery and pleasure recording) seem theoretically indicated.

Insight

Consideration of the concept of "insight" is crucial to any discussion of the management of psychosis. Jaspers (1913/1963) believed that "in psychosis there is no lasting or complete insight. . . . Sometimes at the beginning of the process we find considerable insight, the correction of delusions, the proper assessment of voices, etc. . . . but insight of this sort is quite transient" (pp. 421–422). In the International Pilot Study of Schizophrenia (World Health Organization, 1973), "lack of insight" was described as the most frequent symptom, occurring in 97% of the sample of people with acute schizophrenia.

David (1990) in discussing insight in psychosis, suggests three overlapping dimensions:

1. The recognition that the individual has a mental illness.
2. Compliance with treatment.
3. The ability to relabel unusual mental events (delusions and hallucinations) as pathological.

RECOGNITION OF HAVING A MENTAL ILLNESS

Brooks and colleagues (1968) interviewed 68 people with chronic schizophrenia, of whom about one-third denied any mental illness. However, 30 spoke of having "an insanity" or a "nervous breakdown," and 16 clearly identified their illness as schizophrenia. Further evidence is cited by David (1990) that a significant, "perhaps surprising," proportion of patients do appreciate that they have been ill or "had a breakdown."

COMPLIANCE WITH TREATMENT

Insight is frequently used to predict treatment compliance. But, as an example of how complicated the relationship can be, David (1990) describes a patient who sought treatment because of a belief that electricity was building up in his brain and interfering with his thoughts. He consulted a psychiatrist because "they know about the brain and use shock treatment." Similarly, patients may accept medication or hospitalization despite not accepting the fact that they are ill. This paradoxical recognition of insanity, although it may not be complete, was described by Freud:

> Even in conditions so far removed from the reality of the world as hallucinatory confusional states, one learns from patients after their recovery that at the time in some corner of their minds, as they express it, there was a normal person hidden, who watched the hubbub of the illness go past, like a disinterested spectator. (quoted in Crowcroft, 1967, p. 44)

Likewise, Wing (1987) has commented:

> It should be emphasised that hallucinations and delusions can vary in severity. At one extreme they are overwhelming in their impact and dominate behavior. At the other, the individual can choose how far to attend to them or elaborate them or act on them. The extent to which an individual can acquire a degree of "insight" is therefore crucial in management. (p. 16)

RELABELING OF EVENTS AS PATHOLOGICAL

In relation to relabeling of events as pathological phenomena, Sacks and colleagues (1974) have described patients recovering from delusions as passing through three phases: "delusional," "double-awareness," and "nondelusional." All 20 of a group of their patients participating in a research program were found to have developed delusional ideas about the program. For example, the auditory stimulus Sacks et al. used was described by one patient as a "call to battle stations," and the electroencephalograph (to measure brain electrical activity) was interpreted as a device for reading patients' minds.

Sacks et al. describe how the emergence of reality testing into a delusional situation creates "double awareness." In this phase, a patient becomes increasingly able to establish distance from the delusions and is no longer totally immersed in them. He either questions his delusions or simultaneously accepts and rejects them. Often he may conceal them or in other ways may try to suppress them. The patient is still delusional, but increasingly recognizes the delusions as a symptom that something is wrong with him. This is accompanied by an increasing capacity to relate to people and to utilize their support for his (still impaired) reality testing.

Rakfeldt and Strauss (1989) describe the "low turning point" as a control mechanism in the course of mental disorder. Self-reports are consistent with theories stating that control mechanisms are important. One patient said, "I have a very strong observing ego and I was fascinated and encouraged to think of my mind having that power to step away from the craziness, to look at it and understand it" (p. 32). Rakfeldt and Strauss investigated 28 patients of varied diagnosis and described three phases:

1. An initial rigid focus on one way of dealing with life (e.g., working); the sequence began with increasingly maladaptive coping and desperate efforts to deal with stressors, which led to increasing tension and frustration.
2. Relinquishment of the rigid focus and decompensation.
3. Reorganization of important components of the patients' lives, and development of more diverse modes of dealing with life's activities; the capacity to self-

reflection developed (i.e., detachment), as well as the ability to assume the roles of others.

Breier and Strauss (1983) describe "self-control in psychotic disorders" as occurring in three phases among the patients they studied:

1. The patients became aware of the existence of psychotic and prepsychotic behavior by self-monitoring. In this and the next phase, detecting early affective (i.e., mood-related) signals that might herald the onset of psychosis was particularly important. The "target behaviors" selected included both affective states and psychotic symptoms, but some patients also identified affective symptoms that they believed preceded psychosis and focused on controlling them.
2. Self-evaluation developed as the patients recognized that the implications of these behaviors were particularly important. Some subjects relied on others for help in such evaluations. In some, identification of the state was enough to reduce it; in most who developed insight, however, the third phase was necessary.
3. Mechanisms of self-control were then employed (similar to coping strategies). These included self-instructions (similar to those described by Meichenbaum & Cameron, 1973— e.g., "Act like an adult," "Be responsible"), reduced involvement in activity (e.g., relaxing, isolating oneself at work), or, conversely, increased involvement in activity ("keeping busy" to reduce hallucinations and delusions).

Breier and Strauss also discuss why self-control methods sometimes failed and conclude that there may have been a failure to appreciate emerging symptoms or a misevaluation of them. On some occasions, patients found the symptoms pleasant, or they offered relief from severe psychological distress. They were also concerned that use of medication might obscure recognition of early signs.

Fisher and Winkler (1975) have described one patient's method of attempting to develop "self-control over intrusive experiences." Although she did not have classical schizophrenia, their patient described very distressing visual experiences (seeing heads of screaming dogs and cats, perceptual distortion, and flashes of colors and lights). She felt little control over these sensations and expressed the belief that she was going mad. She was trained by her therapist to bring on the sensations and then dismiss them. This eventually reduced their incidence dramatically and removed the anxiety attached to them.

Finally, Levy and colleagues (1975) have described "integration" and "sealing over" as styles of recovery from acute psychosis. For "recovery" to occur, they quote Freud (1961):

> the illness itself must no longer seem to [the patient] contemptible, but must become an enemy worthy of his mettle, a piece of his personality, which has solid ground for its existence and out of which things of value for his future life have to be derived. (p. 152)

In "sealing over," treatment is aimed at rapid resolution of social functioning, which is believed to provide the best chance of avoiding the deteriorating effects of psychosis; ideally, this ameliorates disintegrative anxiety and leads to psychotic symptoms' being "sealed over." In "integration," the aims are to understand psychotic symptoms and to integrate them into a continuous life experience. These styles are not distinct, but constitute the endpoints of a continuum. Patients who seal over are disinclined to discuss their psychotic symptoms, lack awareness of details of them, and fail to place their psychosis in a personal context. This may lead to distancing and lack of assertiveness in relationships. Integration, although appearing more desirable and resulting in "fuller" insight, may create a vulnerability to relapse because it brings to the surface anxieties and depression, which may then overwhelm patients.

CONCLUSIONS

It is rare that insight in schizophrenia is completely lost. Many patients recognize that they have a mental illness, and can sometimes even clearly identify it as schizophrenia. If not, they often can accept that they have had a "breakdown" or at least that "something is wrong." Even when they fail to accept this, they may still accept treatment, including medication. Some may retain or develop sufficient insight to recognize hallucinations and even, paradoxically, delusions for what they are. Developing control over their illness through such insight can reduce their distress and its damaging effect on their behavior. This is an appropriate aim for therapeutic intervention.

Fears

FEARS OF MADNESS

Freud is quoted as saying, "I always find it uncanny when I can't understand someone in terms of myself" (Crowcroft, 1967, p. 21); he particularly related this to psychosis. Crowcroft (1967) amplified this observation, noting that

> the psychotic's behavior . . . is very far from everyday life. He makes poor contact with others and is withdrawn, living in a world of his own. The glimpses he shows us of his world, as he answers voices we cannot hear, or suffers from punishments we do not understand, frighten us. (pp. 21–22)

What Crowcroft also recognized, although it seems to be frequently forgotten, is that such voices and punishments may frighten the recipient at least as much as they do us. He commented that

> young people, especially intelligent ones, developing schizophrenia, may become depressed as a reaction to their unnerving symptoms. . . . The fear of madness itself can add to the distresses already multiplying and some young patients will respond to their new inner experiences with intense anxiety. (p. 40)

Hirsch and Jolley (1989) have described a "dysphoric syndrome" in schizophrenia and its implications for relapse. They studied 54 patients who had been free of florid psychotic symptoms for at least 6 months. They gave the patients and their families a brief training session about schizophrenia and early signs of relapse. The patients were then randomly assigned to receive treatment (an antipsychotic drug, fluphenazine, given by depot injection) or a placebo. Over the trial period, three-quarters of the placebo group, compared to one-quarter of the treatment group, developed neurotic symptoms (the "dysphoric syndrome") sufficient to cause measurable distress. Eleven relapses occurred, preceded on eight occasions by demonstrable neurotic symptoms. The authors note: "The most frequent symptom emergent on the Early Signs Questionnaire [which Hirsch and Jolley used to detect the neurotic symptoms] at the onset of episodes [was] the subjective fear of 'going crazy'" (p. 49).

Paradoxically, the fear of going mad seems to be related to its precipitation. A spiral of increasing anxiety may be set up, which culminates in a psychotic breakdown. Medication would seem to be prophylactic in reducing the occurrence of these dysphoric symptoms, and also perhaps the rate at which such a spiral builds up.

FEARS OF VIOLENCE

Families and the general population frequently express fears of violence in relation to schizophrenia. And patients themselves may express similar fears of losing control and harming someone inadvertently.

Lindqvist and Allebeck (1990) have reviewed studies in the Netherlands and the United States; they have concluded that individuals with schizophrenia contribute very little to crime in general, and that rates of crime are largely independent of mental disorder when demographic and certain life factors are taken into account. However, this contrasts with the British study of Taylor and Gunn (1984), which did demonstrate some increase in violent crime in a prison as opposed to a community population. Using data from the Central Swedish Police Register on 644 patients with schizophrenia discharged from hospitals in 1971, Lindqvist and Allebeck found the crime rate over the following 15 years to be almost the same as that for the general population in males, but twice as high in females. The rate of violent offenses was four times higher, but these offenses were almost exclusively of minor severity: The authors found 20 cases of assault, the most serious being one of aggravated assault.

Although this study demonstrates some increase in violent crime among schizophrenics as compared to the general population, the absolute incidence is remarkably low (1 serious and 19 minor episodes in 644 patients over 15 years). Violence to the self is a far more reasonable concern, in view of the much higher rates of suicide among schizophrenics than in the community as a whole. This particularly seems to occur in cases where insight is developing and where hopelessness prevails.

The likelihood that a person with schizophrenia will do violent harm to persons other than himself at any one time is therefore very low. Yet the prospect of violence can frequently dominate the concerns of all involved. Indeed, the heightened tension may make it more rather than less likely to occur, thus creating a self-fulfilling prophecy.

FEARS FOR THE FUTURE

Patients and families are virtually always concerned about the patients' future, often to the point of obsessive preoccupation. If they conceptualize the patients' problems as an illness, they generally want to know how much it will interfere with their lives. It may take time for them to express this concern, and they may jump to the conclusion that having schizophrenia means little or no chance of recovery (i.e., that they or their relatives have "dementia praecox"). This overwhelmingly gloomy view of schizophrenia is shared by many professionals and the general population.

Murray (1984) reviewed prognostic factors in schizophrenia and noted that Kraepelin "implied that the vast majority of cases proceeded to a chronic stage. He remained sceptical that full recovery was possible in schizophrenia without any residual defect" (p. 35). However, Murray concluded that "the ensuing years have demonstrated that the outlook is not so bleak" (p. 35). He described Mayer-Gross's 16-year follow-up study published in 1932, in which over a third made social recoveries. He also noted that Brown and colleagues in 1966 were able to report that 56% of people initially hospitalized with schizophrenia made a social recovery; 35% were socially damaged but were able to live in the community; and only 11% were still chronically hospitalized. Bleuler (1974), following a cohort of 208 patients over more than 20 years, made the important observation that on average the patients showed little deterioration after 5 years; if anything, they started to improve.

However, MacMillan and colleagues (1986) followed up 253 patients from different centers with a first episode of schizophrenia. They found that 60% had relapsed in 2 years and that 17 did not even achieve discharge over the period. They concluded that outcome at an early stage was poor for many patients. The same group (Johnstone et al., 1984) attempted to trace 120 patients discharged from hospital over 5–9 years. Only 66, however, were interviewed because of deaths, inability to trace, or unwillingness to cooperate. Of these 66, 18% were considered recovered, but more than 50% continued to demonstrate definite psychotic features. Moreover, 27% had no contact with medical or social services; a further 14% saw only community nurses; and 24% saw only their general practitioners. The authors commented on the inadequacy of community follow-up, but noted that the patients were "discharged at a time when discharge policies were generally less active than at present" (p. 586).

In contrast, Watt and colleagues (1983), in a prospective study of 121 patients over 5 years, followed up all but 1. They found that 48% of the cohort and 58% of new admissions (those without a history of schizophrenia) had a good outcome; 23% of the new admissions had no further episodes. Females fared significantly better than males. The authors noted that the good follow-up may have been the reason for the better-than-usual results. In other words, they suggested that those who do well are usually disproportionately lost to follow-up. Such persons are also forgotten by their therapists, who spend more time seeing those who are most ill and may fail to appreciate the distorting effect this has on their view of prognosis.

Similar quite positive results have been found in much longer studies; Ciompi (1984), reviewing them, suggests that the long term prognosis of schizophrenia is considerably better than hitherto supposed. Services with a long tradition of rehabilitation activity (e.g., Vermont State Psychiatric Service) (Harding et al., 1989) have demonstrated particularly good results.

Of particular importance in sustaining hope are the instances of recovery found in these follow-up studies, even after many years of debilitating illness. As mentioned previously, Strauss (1989) describes the occurrence in some patients of a long period when little improvement appears to occur while "healing" and readjustment take place. This plateau is then followed by progressive improvement. Prognosis cannot be predicted precisely. Undoubtedly a minority become markedly disabled, though few become permanently hospitalized, some struggle along, some cope well, and some recover fully. What is clear is that schizophrenia is not "dementia praecox."

CONCLUSIONS

Fears of violence, fears for the future, and fears of madness itself dominate thinking about schizophrenia by the general population, as well as patients, caregivers and even professionals. Serious violence is rare and does not occur at strikingly higher rates than in the general population. The unfortunate term "dementia praecox" still dominates thinking but is not supported by long-term studies. Schizophrenia has a variable course; even when patients have been institutionalized for years, remarkable changes can still occur. Those patients lost to follow-up by many studies are probably the ones doing disproportionately well. The fear of madness seems paradoxically to be a factor in its development (or at least in relapse), feeding a "vicious cycle." Techniques of "decatastrophization" for dealing with these fears are discussed in Part II.

Psychological Treatment in Schizophrenia

PSYCHODYNAMIC PSYCHOTHERAPY

A full review of the application of psychodynamic psychotherapy to schizophrenia is beyond the scope of this book (for such a review, see Arieti, 1974). However, some mention is necessary to set in context the development of cognitive approaches.

Both Freud (Crowcroft, 1967) and Jaspers (1913/1963) appeared to believe that delusions are wholly insulated from "corrective" information. However, Rudden et al. (1982) have questioned these assumptions that patients hold delusions with absolute fixity, and therefore that psychotherapy has no part to play in their management. They note that the psychiatric literature has endorsed treatment approaches based on this understanding of fixity, such as the following:

1. Ignoring the delusional content and focusing discussion on conflict-free areas.
2. Exploring the patient's delusional beliefs and experiential world to gain information and form an alliance.
3. Participating in the delusion.

Confronting the delusion, they note, is opposed by many authors as futile, if not dangerous. However, they then refer to Federn's caution that not confronting the psychotic individual may constitute "unwitting deception."

Sullivan (1962) warned that avoiding discussion of reality

could be frightening to the patient, who could interpret this as confirmation of his "dangerous ideas." Boverman is quoted as advocating explicit initial statements defining the patient's illness, and specifically mentioning the delusions, to aid in reality testing. So, although Freud did not believe that psychodynamic methods (specifically, psychoanalysis) could be used for treating the psychotic patient, Sullivan (1962), Fromm-Reichmann (1953), Federn (1952), Arieti (1974), and others have attempted to adapt such techniques. However, the dogmatism of many practitioners has not been translated into demonstrably effective practice, and extravagant claims for "the psychogenesis of schizophrenia" (Kind, 1966) have led to a situation where individual psychodynamic psychotherapy is generally considered to be contraindicated in schizophrenia.

Nevertheless Sullivan (1962), with his description of "schizophrenia as a human process," was undoubtedly influential in promoting "normalization" and the importance of interpersonal relationships in therapy. With his "direct analysis," Rosen (1953) was noted in his day to be a particularly successful therapist. He based his therapy on the dream psychology of Freud because of the similarity between psychotic and dream material: "What is psychosis but an interminable nightmare in which the wishes are so well disguised that the psychotic does not awaken? Why not then awaken the psychotic by unmasking the real content of his psychosis?" (p. 4).

The governing principle of direct analysis was that the therapist must be an omnipotent protector and provider for his patient:

> When the patient is mute, he is generally rigid. In that case, it must be understood that what the patient is saying is "I am frightened stiff." You have to tell him what you see or hear him to be saying so that somewhere inside of him, he will gain the sense that he is no longer alone; he is understood. Somebody is trying to help. (p. 13)

Rosen suggested "oral interpretations," although many of these seemed to be remarkably obscure. However, the intensity of the relationships he developed with patients comes across in his writings. Rosen also described the use of "recovered" patients as aides in the treatment of others according to an intensive model (treating one patient at a time). This demonstration that he valued patients' contributions, and the self-help element he incorporated, may have been important factors in the process of treatment.

After uncertainty and counterargument over the next three decades, the Boston Collaborative Study (Stanton et al., 1984), a controlled trial of the use of two types of psychotherapy in schizophrenia, seemed to settle the issue of whether it could be demonstrated to be effective or not. Carpenter (1984) commented that "the results support the view [demon-

TABLE 13.1. Description of Therapies Compared in the Boston Collaborative Study

	Reality-adaptive supportive	Exploratory insight-oriented
1. Objectives	Symptom relief via drug management and strengthening of existing defenses	Self-understanding: how one feels and thinks, and how these influence the course of one's life
2. Interview focus	Management, complaints, interpersonal problems, current situational problems	Relationship to therapist and significant others, exploration of feelings and conflicts
3. Psychic arena	Focus on current awareness, no hidden agendas	Look for current meanings, hidden motivation, unconscious
4. Temporal focus	Present and future	Present and past
5. Techniques	Support, reassurance, limits, clarification, direction, suggestions for environmental manipulation, use of community resources	Support, reassurance, limits, clarification, interpretation, catharsis
6. Transference	Encourage positive to further alliance, actively discourage negative	Accept positive and work through negative
7. Counter-transference	Positive feelings important and expressible, control negative	Mixed feelings expected and generally not disclosed

Note. Adapted from Stanton et al. (1984).

strated in earlier studies] . . . that supportive psychotherapy is at least as effective as more intensive psychotherapy based on psychoanalytic theory and psychodynamic practice." (p. 599).

However, the study (Stanton et al., 1984) compared exploratory insight-oriented therapy against reality-adaptive supportive therapy. The latter was considerably more than simply "supportive" (see Table 13.1); indeed, it resembled cognitive therapy in its emphasis on the present, symptom relief, reality testing, and problem solving. Significant differences were found (Gunderson et al., 1984) in days hospitalized (at least in the first year, with a continuing trend in the second), and advantages were also noted in relation to "recidivism" and role performance. There does therefore appear to be some evidence that more directive, reality-oriented techniques may be worthy of further exploration.

In summary, there is no adequate evidence from clinical trials that demonstrates beneficial effects for psychodynamic psychotherapy in schizophrenia. However, there is some evidence (particularly from the Boston Collaborative Study) that more structured, reality-oriented techniques may be effective.

COGNITIVE THERAPY

The use of cognitive therapy in schizophrenia was first described by Beck in 1952. He encouraged a person with chronic schizophrenia to scrutinize the appearance and behavior of alleged FBI agents who were visiting his shop, in order to reality-test his belief that these persons had him under surveillance. The patient succeeded in narrowing down his original group of 50 "suspects" to 2–3 possibilities, and reported that he felt he would soon be able to "eliminate them completely." Despite the existence of the delusion for 7 years, it proved modifiable: "Although not all of its aspects can be traced back to their origins, the patient provided enough clues to explain many of its elements . . . despite the longstanding nature of the delusion it proved to be interpretable to the patient" (Hole, Rush, & Beck, 1979, p. 311). Hole et al. (1979) commented: "The combination of tracing the antecedents of the delusion, and helping the patient to test his conclusions systematically, helped him to recognize and to gradually do away with the irrational and rigid belief-system" (312–313).

Hole, Rush, and Beck (1979) asked eight delusional inpatients to discuss the nature of their delusional beliefs and the evidence supporting them. They were interviewed within 48 hours of admission, and hour-long interviews were conducted every 2–3 days thereafter; on average, seven interviews were conducted with each patient. The first interview was used to generate approximately 10 statements, which were rated in terms of strength of belief from 0% to 100%. Then changes in ratings and reasons for these changes were derived from subsequent interviews. Hole et al. defined four dimensions for measuring delusions:

1. Conviction.
2. Accommodation (the degree to which a delusion could be modified by external events or incongruities).
3. Pervasiveness (the percentage of the day spent ruminating about delusional concerns, seeking delusional goals, or interpreting experience in terms of delusional systems).
4. Encapsulation (the extent to which a decrease in pervasiveness could occur without an associated decrement in conviction).

Hole et al. found that half of the patients showed no change; the other half showed reduced pervasiveness, and half of these also showed decreased conviction. They concluded: "We suggest that delusions may function in much the same way as other beliefs and convictions. Delusions may differ from other beliefs only quantitatively with respect to how easily they can be modified by external events" (p. 313).

Watts and colleagues (1973) described their attempts at modification of abnormal beliefs. Their focus was on "paranoid beliefs" in paranoid schizophrenia; such a belief was defined broadly as any abnormal belief of a paranoid schizophrenic that contributed in some way to his social isolation. They described two main classes:

1. Mistaken beliefs about the subject's own appearance.
2. Mistaken beliefs about other people's actions or intentions toward him.

Watts et al. noted that confrontation of such beliefs could result in "psychological reactance," whereby the original opinion would become more firmly held or even more extreme. Their intention therefore was to minimize the "reactance" in the following ways:

1. The less strongly held beliefs were targeted first, unless specific themes bound beliefs together. The rationale for this was similar to that for systematic desensitization.

2. Direct confrontation was avoided. The therapist did not explicitly require the subject to abandon his own beliefs and adopt those of the therapist. "It was therefore made clear that the subject was only being asked to consider the facts and arguments discussed with him, and to entertain possible alternative beliefs" (p. 360).

3. To facilitate this indirect approach, discussion was centered not on the belief itself, but on the subject's evidence for it.

4. The therapist encouraged the subject himself to voice the arguments against his own beliefs, even if quite direct questioning was necessary to achieve this.

Their results demonstrated that belief modification with graded re-exposure to avoided social circumstances was successful in mediating the intensity of beliefs significantly.

Milton and colleagues (1978) compared confrontation (of a reasonably judicious nature) against belief modification, as described above, in persistently deluded patients. They studied 16 patients and demonstrated a significant fall in the strength of delusions in both groups, but no significant difference between groups in this respect. Social anxiety was reduced in the belief modification group.

Greenwood (1984) described the use of cognitive therapy with a group of "young adult chronic patients." He outlined three stages of therapy. The first had an explicit agenda of securing the patient's involvement in treatment; the second, or "socialization," phase was intended to facilitate the patient's understanding of the cognitive therapy process; the third consisted of the application of specific cognitive and behavioral techniques. Greenwood used these techniques with a small group of patients over a 10-month period, but unfortunately did not describe the results of the intervention.

Rudden et al. (1982) presented three case histories suggesting that patients do not always hold delusional ideas as tenaciously as has been claimed, and that reality-"clarifying" techniques seemed useful.

Hartman and Cashman (1983) described the use of cognitive–behavioral and psychopharmacological treatment of delusional symptoms. They defined "delusions" as

> fixed cognitive processes which are not amenable to rational explanation. Pragmatic flexibility in thought is constricted and the individual resists changing cognitive schemes even when confronted with contradictory evidence. In Piagetian terms, these patients have an "accommodation" deficit. That is, they fail to change perceptual operations or construct new schemes in order to incorporate new objects or experiences. (p. 50)

Their technique involved belief modification, together with exposure, response prevention, and other behavioral techniques. Their aim was for patients to achieve a sense of mastery, control, and then self-efficacy. Hartman and Cashman described three patients—two males (one preoccupied with the size of his head, the other with homosexuality) and one female (who was deluded that women around her were homosexual and making overtures to her). Diagnostic criteria for schizophrenia were not defined, and there must be some doubt as to whether all three patients had schizophrenia. A crossover design with an antipsychotic drug (pimozide) was used, and at least two of the patients improved. The first patient's delusional beliefs improved with the drug, and then his depressive symptoms improved with cognitive therapy when he was crossed over. The other male patient improved with cognitive therapy prior to crossing over to the drug treatment.

Perris (1988) has described in detail the theoretical background for the use of cognitive therapy by his team in Umea, Sweden. His approach has roots in psychodynamic psychotherapy, particularly the cognitive–volitional school of Arieti (1974), although divergence from it is commented upon. He distinguishes between cognitive and behavior therapy, seeing these as differing fundamentally, in contrast to Beck's view. He does nevertheless propose that therapists should discuss hypotheses with patients rather than make interpretations to them, and he advocates classical behavior therapy techniques such as the use of homework. His approach is warm and receptive, and he agrees with Arieti (1974) that

> it is the responsibility of the therapist to take the initiative in conversation in such a way that contact is unmistakeable. However it is important in this context to be extremely receptive to every form of non-verbal contact from the patient and to ensure that the patient is truly able to feel understood. (p. 119)

Perris (1988) discusses individual vulnerability, but writes of moving "from the 'schizophrenogenic mother' to the 'schizophrenogenic family' and beyond." He describes the use of these terms which could be considered quite derogatory; however, he also considers evidence that distortion by patients, even "anti-parental zeal," may be a contributing factor to the negative picture attributed to mothers (though not fathers, as he notes). He talks of life events as possible triggering factors, but does not discuss the literature in any detail. He reviews the literature on perceived "locus of control" and concludes that generally patients have a more external locus than nonpatients (i.e., a greater tendency to refer control to others rather than themselves). He does, however, note that some research has suggested that although patients may not believe they have control over their own thoughts or behavior, they may at the same time be convinced of their ability to control others by act of will.

Perris's description of the practical use of cognitive therapy is divided into two parts: milieu therapy within small therapeutic communities, and individual therapy. He admits patients to the former for "intensive holistic" treatment. However, specific patient data are lacking in his book. Some such data have been presented to the World Congress of Cognitive Therapy (Andersson et al., 1989), but unfortunately these pertained to a group of patients of mixed diagnosis admitted to the communities since their establishment in 1986, and so specific conclusions about the communities' effectiveness in schizophrenia are difficult to draw.

Fowler and Morley (1989) recently described the cognitive–behavioral treatment of five patients. Their intervention included the following elements:

1. Attempts to change patients' beliefs about their "voices" through belief modification (as described by Watts et al., 1973).
2. Bringing on and dismissing hallucinations in sessions (as described by Fisher & Winkler, 1975).
3. Instruction in coping strategies (basically, focusing patients' attention on the external stimuli causing symptom onset).

Four of the patients reported an increase in ability to control hallucinations, but only one also reported decreased frequency of hallucinations and reduced belief in the reality of them.

Brenner (1989) and colleagues have described a different form of cognitive therapy, which focuses on "the treatment of basic psychological dysfunctions from a systemic point of view" (p. 74). They have investigated "the processes intervening between the critical stress experienced by vulnerable persons and the emergence of their manifest symptoms" (p. 74). They hypothesize that the lowered tolerance threshold is essentially a result of specific dysfunctions in information processing. People with schizophrenia have dysfunctions or deficits in all stages of information processing—attention, memory, and conceptualization. Brenner's group has developed an "integrated psychological treatment program" that provides training in information processing and social skills for patients. Five consecutive subprograms are used: cognitive differentiation, social perception, verbal communication, social skills, and interpersonal problem solving. Evaluation studies (quoted in Brenner, 1989) have demonstrated the program's efficacy in chronic schizophrenia but generalization to nontreatment settings has not yet been clearly demonstrated.

Lowe and Chadwick (1990) have recently described the successful use of a "verbal challenge" technique (essentially based on cognitive therapy) with two patients who were encouraged to develop alternatives to their delusional beliefs in an "atmosphere of collaborative empiricism."

In summary, the progress of research into cognitive therapy in schizophrenia has been marked by sporadic outbursts of activity since Beck first described its use. Generally, studies have involved relatively small numbers of patients, but some have demonstrated promising results. Brenner and associates have been most thorough in their use of controlled evaluation of their techniques, but their results have been limited by generalizability. Over the past 3 years, more and more studies based on Beck's conception of cognitive therapy have been published (Kingdon & Turkington, 1991b).

USE OF A "NORMALIZING" RATIONALE WITH COGNITIVE THERAPY

We have recently described the application of a "normalizing" rationale with the use of cognitive therapy (Kingdon & Turkington, 1991a). We provide a more detailed description of this approach in Part II of this book. Our study included 64 patients (see Table 13.2). These patients satisfied appropriate research criteria (Spitzer et al., 1975; World Health Organization, 1989) for schizophrenia.

The patients were all retrospectively identified from the clinical caseload of Kingdon, a general adult psychiatrist working wholly within the British National Health Service from a district general hospital. Forty-five of the patients were inherited from Kingdon's predecessor in 1984. These therefore represented a complete cross-section of patients with schizo-

TABLE 13.2. Characteristics of Patient Sample (*n* = 64)

Age (mean)	40.4 (range = 20–72) years
Length of illness (mean)	12.1 years
Admission to hospitals over period	
Number of admissions (mean)	1.74
Total weeks (mean)	13.5
Number receiving medication	46 (72%)
Average amount (in those receiving it)	249 mg[a]

Note. No suicides/homicides over 7-year period.

[a]Chlorpromazine equivalent.

phrenia, from ones newly diagnosed with acute episodes to ones who had spent 30–40 years in a mental hospital. There was one other general psychiatrist working in the district to provide comprehensive coverage but there was not a separately designated rehabilitation or forensic service.

Although the techniques we have described (see Kingdon & Turkington, 1991a, and Part II of this book) would seem to have been of therapeutic value, the setting in which they have been used must also be commented upon. Bassetlaw District Nottinghamshire is a semirural district in the English Midlands, which has a population of 103,000 focused on two towns and a variety of villages. It is demographically average on most population indicators, but has unemployment above average and a below-average proportion of individuals from ethnic minorities. Prior to 1984, psychiatric services were based in Saxondale Hospital, a mental hospital located 30 miles away (outside the city of Nottingham). A psychiatrist and social worker visited the district to do outpatient clinics and visit patients in their own homes. A local authority day center opened in 1976.

In 1984, a district service was established in active collaboration with local authority and voluntary agencies; this new service emphasized community mental health and "normalization" principles. It consisted of a district general hospital unit, hospital hostels that provided 24-hour nursing care for those who required it after the mental hospital closed, and a range of other residential provisions (Kingdon et al., 1991; Turkington et al., 1990). Facilities in the community were developed, including a crisis intervention flat (Turkington et al., 1991), social support groups (Pym, 1989), and a "befriending" scheme (Kingdon et al., 1989). Independent evaluation before and after the development of these facilities (Ferguson, 1990) demonstrated significant improvement in general practitioner opinion of the service. An overall appraisal of the service was published in the *British Medical Journal* (Groves, 1990).

It was therefore a well-developed service in which to use our techniques. Facilities and community staff were available to provide a variety of alternatives to admission. When a patient did require admission to a hospital, he was admitted to a modern district general hospital unit or a hostel. Admission was seen as an appropriate management policy, essential in some circumstances and useful in others. Because of the nature of the facilities available, avoidance of admission did not need to be set as a goal at which to aim, and thus admission was not construed in any way as failure. Concomitant with this, ward staff members did not seem to see their roles as any less significant than those more directly working in community settings. In such a service, "decatastrophization" (reducing fear associated with schizophrenia and hospitalization, see Part II) was much easier than if a large, remote mental hospital had been the only available admission option.

Our study (Kingdon & Turkington, 1991a) has suggested that our treatment program may be efficacious. At the end of the 5-year initial study period, only four patients had been inpatients throughout the period, and for most of that period they had been residents in a hospital hostel on the fringes of the district general hospital site. Although most were symptomatically improved, one required physical care in addition to psychiatric care (for severe epilepsy); two continued to require staff support; and one did not wish to leave, although not requiring the level of nursing care provided. Of the remainder, the average number of admissions was 1.74 for a mean total length of stay of 13.5 weeks (see Table 13.2). None of the 19 diagnosed during the period remained hospitalized. The accommodation and employment status of the group are graphically depicted in Figure 13.1. Eleven were "housewives," 15 were employed, 2 were physically handicapped, and 36 were unemployed. Fifteen attended day centers.

The techniques have also proved safe to use. There have been no suicides or homicides over the period of the study (or since its completion—i.e., over a 7-year period), and incidents of aggressive behavior have been infrequent and minor (indeed, they have lessened over that period). We have reported an audit relating to the use of a nonseclusion policy in the district general hospital unit as a whole (Kingdon & Bakewell, 1988). This involved contact with community agencies, probation, police, the local remand prison, and secure hospital facilities. We confirmed that patients were not being excluded from the unit because of the treatment policies in use; on the contrary, all personnel were positive about the development of these policies. Further follow-up of the group is occurring, and this information will be presented in due course.

Demonstrating success, however, also involves controlled evaluation, and a pilot study is underway. More complete evaluations will be needed, and proposals are currently being discussed (see "Evaluation and Evolution" at the end of the book).

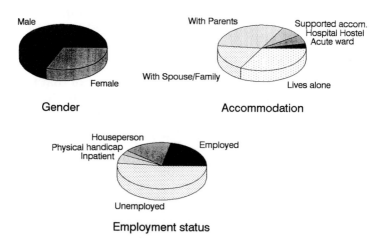

FIGURE 13.1. Breakdown of the patient sample ($n = 64$) by gender and by accommodation and employment status at the end of the study period.

In conclusion, a "normalizing" rationale to explain and "decatastrophize" symptom emergence would appear to be a useful component of a treatment package based on cognitive therapy in the treatment of schizophrenia. Improvements in symptomatology, medication compliance, and social performance appear to occur, but confirmation of this by further controlled investigation remains necessary. This integrated program may yet allow us, and more importantly patients themselves, to begin to understand the sanity of madness.

PROCESS OF THERAPY

To illustrate the use of our techniques, we have interspersed a series of case examples among the descriptions of techniques. (The patients' identities have been fully disguised, and individual symptomatology has been rearranged.) The first example provides a full description of a patient presenting a complex of problems, and details of his management are given. The remainder are briefer and are designed to bring out the use of some specific techniques.

The depth and intensity of therapy that can be pursued with different individuals who have schizophrenia are extremely variable, and this fact is reflected in these examples. Some patients are treated at what may appear to be quite a superficial level; others require more in-depth psychotherapy, involving schema-focused techniques and interpersonal understanding. Our outcome criteria are improvements in depressed, anxious, or confused mood and in functioning—that is, distress and disability—and not whether our repertoire of cognitive techniques has been exhausted. Even improvement in psychotic symptoms per se is seen, in the final eventuality, as of secondary importance to such mood and functional objectives.

Study 1: The Man Who Was Controlled by a Satellite

Bernard is a 57-year-old man who was transferred to our psychiatric unit after having been taken into police custody and incarcerated in prison. He had been living in a corrugated iron shack adjacent to a farmer's field for the previous 3 years, and prior to this had "lived rough" (i.e., lived like a homeless person) for a 10-year period.

On this occasion Bernard had become very agitated when

the farmer's children had left some vegetables at the door of his shed. He smashed the farmer's door, and the police were contacted. Examination of his mental state revealed Bernard to be aloof and hostile (although not aggressive). He was in a state of obvious malnutrition and poor hygiene, with long, unkempt hair and a straggly grey beard. He spoke at a normal rate, without evidence of thought disorder. He denied obsessional thoughts or ritualistic behavior. There was evidence of anxiety, tension, and episodic agitation. He was not overtly depressed, but reported poor sleep, reduced food intake, and episodic suicidal ideation.

Bernard had the paranoid delusion that a satellite was being operated with the purpose of removing the thoughts of people with high intelligence quotients. It was also being used to manipulate "clever people" in various other ways—for example, giving them headaches and stomach pains, interfering with their sleep, making them think certain thoughts, and even causing them to perform certain actions. He blamed the satellite for the farmer's broken door, because it was making his life unbearable and he acted in a state of extreme distress. This was not a passivity phenomenon, as Bernard acknowledged having control over his actions.

At times Bernard "heard" the people who operated the satellite saying things such as "those contemptible scum." They were once "heard" to say, "We can do whatever we like with him." Simpler hallucinations were also heard (e.g., whirring and humming noises), which Bernard attributed to the satellite. Cognitive testing revealed no abnormality.

He had committed a similar offense 4 years previously, resulting in his detention under the Mental Health Act of 1983. On that occasion, despite similar symptoms, he successfully appealed against detention to a mental health tribunal and was released without treatment. The reasons were not given for this decision, but the tribunal appeared to have concluded that his illness was unlikely to respond to treatment. Subsequently, he did not cooperate with attempts to treat him in the community. On this subsequent admission, he again appealed to the tribunal at an early stage in his detention, but this time he was not discharged.

Bernard described a normal birth and development. He had a happy childhood without neurotic or deviant behavior. He tended to be shy and kept to a small circle of close friends. His performance at school was above average, and he left at 17 years of age with several good examination scores. He went on to train as an accountant but, taking little pleasure in this, dropped out of his course and worked at some laboring jobs before emigrating to Australia in 1963. He received full training as a chemist there and worked with a pharmaceutical company for 3 years. At this time a senior post became available, and Bernard started to work excessively hard (including a lot of overtime) in an attempt to improve his chances of promotion. He was, however, unsuccessful in his application and subsequently appealed against this through the courts. He initially won his case, but the decision was subsequently overturned by the appeal court.

There followed a period in which Bernard became very disturbed with general paranoid delusions—"My colleagues were against me and they drugged my tea." The specific delusion about the satellite emerged, accompanied by the auditory hallucinations. He was hospitalized for 4 months and then discharged. Subsequently he returned to England in 1972, determined to take his case to the International Court of Justice at the Hague.

He "lived rough" for a 10-year period and had one brief stay in Wandsworth Prison, London, when he was charged with carrying a lethal weapon. He was seen by a psychiatrist in prison. It emerged that he was sleeping in a park; when he was woken by a police constable, he threatened the officer with a broken bottle, perceiving him to be "a government agent." The case was discharged, but no treatment or follow-up was apparently offered. No further involvement with the police or any treatment agency occurred until he was first admitted to our unit in 1985.

Little was known about the members of Bernard's family, as he had lost contact with them during his time in Australia, but his mother was known to have died of heart problems in 1966 (at approximately the same time that he first developed symptoms). He had a sister who was 4 years older than he. It was believed that his father had died. He described good relationships with both parents. There was no family history of mental illness of any type.

Bernard had no significant medical illnesses, and he did not use alcohol or any illegal drugs. A clear account of his premorbid personality was difficult to obtain, but he had certainly always been a sensitive introvert, tending to be stable in mood and preferring intellectual pastimes. He had never had a girlfriend, but denied homosexual orientation.

At the time of his admission, a definite diagnosis of schizophrenia was made and a treatment plan devised. He was offered chlorpromazine (100 mg four times a day), which he refused for the first few weeks of his stay. He was also offered twice-weekly sessions of cognitive–behavioral therapy with a therapist (Turkington). The psychotherapy notes have been condensed in the following paragraphs to illustrate the main techniques used.

Session 1: Bernard's history was clarified and current sources of stress were explored—for example, "being pressured into taking medication." The session was spent building rapport and sympathizing with his problems in relation to the satellite. Bernard was intermittently abusive during the session and clearly did not trust the therapist.

Session 2: Bernard refused to see the therapist—"that sniveling little git."

Session 3: Bernard again refused to see therapist and was heard by the nursing staff to say, "Oh, no . . . here he comes . . . I'm off."

Session 4: Bernard finally agreed to see the therapist. His main complaints were of poor sleep, auditory hallucinations, and headaches and stomach pains (which he believed to be caused by the satellite). A psychoeducational approach was introduced. Bernard agreed that he had been under a lot of stress recently "because of the satellite," and agreed that people very often get headaches as a result of overwork and the like. He was also able to agree that his abdominal pains felt like hunger pains. These phenomena were eventually accepted as being direct consequences of his agitated and stressed state, rather than being caused in some mysterious way by the satellite.

Bernard was surprised when it was explained to him that it is possible, maybe even probable, for anybody to have hallucinations after going for long enough without sleep. He asked for proof of this. It now seemed sensible to him to take the medication to help him to get a good night's sleep and relax, and thus to cure the headaches. Bernard saw this session as valuable, and he became more eager to see the therapist.

Session 5: In this session, the antecedents of the delusion about the satellite were explored in detail, to help form the basis for more detailed work later and to improve insight. Before beginning the session, Bernard asked whether the lack of sleep in the period leading up to his breakdown could have been an important factor. He agreed that this was likely to have been the case. He was then asked to go through the period in some detail (inductive questioning), and to remember any particular recurring thoughts. "I'm the best ... I should get it [the promotion]" was all he could remember. On rationally weighing up the experience and the qualifications of the other candidates, he was able to agree that it would actually have been a difficult choice as to who was most suitable. He agreed that he had been overworking in an attempt to tip the balance of the decision in his favor, and that out of all this a "nervous breakdown" had occurred, in which he had believed that his colleagues were against him and had drugged his tea. It was significant that Bernard no longer evidenced the extreme emotional investment in this that he had shown previously.

At the end of the session, Bernard asked the therapist whether he believed in the satellite. When the therapist indicated that the satellite was probably another aspect of the same breakdown, Bernard abruptly terminated the interview.

Sessions 6–7: Following the gradual improvement of sessions 4 and 5, there was an increase in stress, manifested in agitation. The therapist was concerned that he had delved too deeply, too quickly. He took a step back from the delusion at this point to help Bernard with his distress. Bernard's tension was explained as a manifestation of anxiety, and he was taught the behavioral principles of progressive muscular relaxation. Some rational responses to his catastrophic thoughts were produced: For example, "The satellite is controlling me and it is hell" was replaced by "I can control my breathing and progressively relax my muscles," in an attempt to show Bernard that he still had a degree of control.

Sessions 8–9: By now Bernard was feeling more settled again, and in these two sessions the central feature of the psychopathology was gently tackled. Unfortunately, Bernard was not agreeable to working with his emotional investment in the delusion, as demonstrated by his anger. This would have been done by using techniques to help Bernard identify automatic thoughts and change them by means of rational responses. A reduction in emotional investment is recommended before working on a delusion. Bernard's belief in the satellite was not confronted as a false belief but approached by "guided discovery," as two scientific investigators would tackle a joint research initiative:

THERAPIST: I think we need to do some work on this satellite issue. It would be a scandal if it were being used in this way.

BERNARD: I'll do everything I can to help bring them [the people operating the satellite] to justice.

T: The more information that you can give us, the better, because I am keen to know how you think it might work.

B: It's electronic.

T: How do you know that?

B: Sometimes I can hear it making a whirring and humming sound.

T: We need more information. . . . Could you keep a diary and record exactly what you hear? How long has it been running for?

B: When it was first designed back in 1967, I was one of the first people it was used on. They stole two ideas that I was about to patent for an electrical generator and an electric engine.

T: Most electronic parts would have run out by now. Do they keep replacing parts?

B: No, they are rogues who run the satellite. They don't have full approval and don't have access to parts.

T: You would expect it to lose power from time to time. Does that ever happen?

B: Yes, but only very occasionally.

T: Can the satellite still reach you from Australia?

B: They must have moved it to Britain. I would expect that it is sited in the Harworth area [near the hospital].

T: Is it possible that other forms of control, like witchcraft or hypnosis, could be used to produce these effects?

B: I still think that a satellite is most likely.

T: Let's decide on the basis of the evidence over the next week. Could you record everything that is done to you and any evidence that there is as to how this could be done?

Session 10: The therapist and Bernard resumed their discussion of the issue:

B: Why don't the psychiatrists take over the satellite? You could potentially do some good with it.

T: Thanks for that suggestion. What has happened to you is certainly remarkable. Did you feel troubled much by the satellite since I last saw you. . . . What have you discovered?

B: There's been less than usual. . . . I can't explain why. Maybe they are having a break (*smiles*). I heard the whirring sound twice and thought that they were starting up, and I asked the charge nurse, but it was only a fan on the wall.

Bernard was by now much more sociable and was interacting with other patients and staff on the ward. He was even seen to smile on occasion.

Session 11: The therapist ventured to probe Bernard's beliefs a little more deeply:

T: You have obviously felt tormented for many years by the satellite. What has been the worst thing about it?

B: It just doesn't give you a minute's peace.

T: What's the worst thing about that?

B: I have had no time to work on my ideas and when I have good ideas—for example, the electric generator—those scum take them from me.

T: If you had been able to work on these ideas, what would have happened?

B: The world would be a much easier place to live in, and I would get the respect I deserve.

T: Which of those two aspects is the most important to you?

B: Having the respect of my colleagues. I should have been given that job (*starts to weep*).

T: I'm sorry to have upset you, but what I'm hearing you say is that you are demanding of yourself that you are a professional success. Is that right?

B: Yes.

Session 12: The therapist continued to explore Bernard's beliefs with him:

T: How do you feel about our last meeting?

B: I didn't enjoy it much.

T: Can we say a little more about that subject?

B: If we need to.

T: What types of success are there?

B: Brilliant ideas, inventions, plays, paintings, things like that.

T: These certainly are, but what percentage of people can be successful in that way?

B: Not many, I suppose.

T: Most of us are just normal people who get successes out of various aspects of life in small ways. We can't all be like Leonardo or Shakespeare, can we?

B: Everybody has some ability.

T: I think we should all measure our successes on a day-to-day basis. For example, managing to be content and reasonably happy might be regarded as a success. Also, writing a letter or going on a trip could be regarded as a success, as it has been years since you have done those things.

B: Most people aren't happy, so your first point is true. But things like writing a letter are just normal things, and to me would only be a step towards a much bigger project.

T: Let's start with some of those simple things, then. Could you write some down for me? [Mastery and pleasure forms (see Beck et al., 1985) were introduced.] I also want you to write me an essay about different types of success.

Sessions 13–15: Gentle disputation was continued about the demand for intellectual success, with various homework exercises.

Bernard had now been discharged from his detention under the Mental Health Act, and as it was felt that he probably would not comply with medication in a hostel setting, the drug was discontinued under controlled circumstances on the ward. He moved to a "Turning Point" hostel for rehabilitation, and at review 6 months later he remained sociable and was interacting well with other residents. He was also finding new ways to occupy his time and was making use of local resources. Staff members felt that his progress was such that he could soon move toward a less supervised setting. He was on occasion angry at the staff, but in general he contained this well. Despite his not being on medication, there was no evidence of active psychosis, and he was not heard to mention the satellite. Then, after about a year in the hostel, he abruptly left after a minor disagreement.

A couple of months later, we were contacted by a social worker from a city 50 miles away. Bernard had presented himself at the local housing department, registered himself as homeless, and had been rehoused in a small bungalow in a village on the outskirts of the city. The social worker had become involved when he had become angry with the local general practitioner. He had presented himself to the general practitioner for a "sickness certificate," but the doctor had refused to give him one, as he could find nothing wrong with him. Bernard's past history was explained to the general practitioner, and the situation was resolved. He is now living independently.

Discussion: This study illustrates the use of cognitive therapy in the treatment of entrenched systematized delusions (see "Delusions," below). It was useful in engaging Bernard in the assessment process (see "Assessment," below) and then in treatment by its nonconfrontational nature; it also encouraged collaboration between the therapist and patient in investigating symptom data. The therapeutic alliance was difficult to establish because Bernard was so hostile and suspicious, but once established, it was strong enough to allow work on very sensitive issues.

The therapist kept to his agenda and was not deterred by the hostility directed at him, although he took due regard of it. Psychoeducational work (see "Explanations," below) helped Bernard to develop an understanding of what seemed to be happening to him and laid the basis, at least transiently, for the rational acceptance of medication (see "Medication," below). Explaining that similar symptoms to those he was experiencing have been demonstrated under conditions of stress caused by sleep deprivation (Oswald, 1974) helped Bernard toward an understanding of why his symptoms might have emerged as they did.

Detailed retrospective investigation, through inductive questioning, of the antecedents of symptom emergence seemed to be an important step in therapy. Although this investigation reactivated Bernard's anxiety, it probably improved his insight and motivated him. It was important to retreat on occasion. Tactical withdrawal (see "Tactical Withdrawal," below) was prudent when Bernard's symptoms seemed about to flare up, as after session 5. It was vital that the length of sessions was kept flexible, to the extent of omitting them altogether or replacing them with nonthreatening maneuvers (e.g., supportive psychotherapy or relaxation).

The therapist initially approached the core symptoms gently and sympathetically, using standard cognitive therapy techniques. Tackling core symptoms is easier when the surrounding emotional investment can be dealt with helping the patient to form rational responses and work with them. This proved most difficult with Bernard. Certainly confrontation or any hint of it was avoided as far as possible, as this would only have led to hostility and disruption of the fragile rapport being built. Insight came gradually, and it would have been counterproductive to delve deeply. Much more important targets were Bernard's distress and social isolation, both of which improved despite the persistence of his delusional beliefs.

It proved useful to find the underlying schema from which Bernard's delusion appeared to have developed, and this was done by inference chaining. It became clear that Bernard held a grandiose schema demanding professional success. When this pervading conception of himself was invalidated, despite considerable effort at work and lack of sleep in his bid for promotion, the paranoid delusion emerged. It did, however, appear understandable in relation to his situation and his personality. This to some extent may explain Bernard's marked emotional investment in the delusion and the tenacity with which he held it. Although the delusion was resistant to direct negotiation, the irrational beliefs around it were open to the standard treatment techniques that Ellis (1962) and Beck and colleagues (1979, 1985, 1990) have described.

The delusional system seemed to weaken with reduction in the emotional investment in it, such that Bernard gradually discontinued voicing and acting upon it. He was not, however, confronted directly to assess whether the delusion remained, and we consider this to be contraindicated until a few more years have passed. Relapse was quite likely when he discontinued the medication, which is why it was discontinued in a controlled environment. However this has not yet occurred and is an argument in favor of the benefit of cognitive therapy to Bernard.

PREREQUISITE EXPERIENCE

Four basic requirements for the use of these techniques by individual practitioners are as follows:

1. Practitioners should have broad clinical experience with working with psychotic patients. In the future, these techniques may be adapted for use as part of initial training program, however until their use has been more extensively investigated, they can be recommended (with caution) only for experienced practitioners.

2. A sound practical knowledge of the use of cognitive and behavior therapy techniques in anxiety and depression is necessary:

a. Such techniques form the framework on which the following description is built.

b. They are also essential in their own right for treatment of the anxiety and depression that occur with such frequency in this patient group.

3. The use of the present techniques is part of a multidisciplinary management program complementing, and not supplanting, appropriate pharmacological and rehabilitation measures. Familiarity with such measures is therefore necessary.

4. The theoretical background to the use of the techniques as described in Part I should be studied.

ASSESSMENT

Full psychiatric, psychological, and social assessment in the conventional manner is necessary, with exclusion or parallel management of physical pathology. Psychiatric assessment to determine the target signs and symptoms is clearly an intrinsic part of attempts to resolve them. However, though diagnostic psychopathology (e.g., Schneiderian first-rank symptoms or research criteria) is essential, eliciting other signs and symptoms (e.g., visual hallucinations, anxiety and depressive symptoms) should not be neglected.

Assessing the Patient's Personal and Family Background

Although the focus of therapy is on cognitions and behaviors that are occurring in the "here and now," their development over the period of the illness and the prodromal (preceding) period requires investigation. This is placed in a holistic context by the usual thorough assessment of the personal and family background.

Such assessments, in our experience, can be made at a very early period in the patient's psychotic illness. It is unusual to find patients who on initial presentation cannot give the essential facts of their personal background. Indeed, most appreciate the importance of doing so and are frequently distracted from their psychotic symptomatology while history details are elicited. It may be necessary to bring them gently, patiently, but persistently "back to the point" when they move off it; however, this can be therapeutic in itself.

In patients with whom this is not possible, or patients who have longer or more complex histories, supplementary information from relatives, friends, and clinical notes can be invaluable. Attempts to obtain such information should be made with all patients, subject to their informed consent.

Determining Significant Life Events and Circumstances

Patients vary considerably in their ability to identify life events or circumstances of significance in the development of their symptoms. The personal and social history assessment can act as a useful "sieve," clarifying for the therapist and patient significant areas. The process by which "pressure points" emerge appears to be therapeutic in itself. Confirmation by the therapist that, for example, work or family concerns have

explanatory potential for the patient can begin to bring meaning to the patient's confusing experiences.

Discussing the patient's life circumstances at the time of
onset and the "buildup" period to it is an essential early stage
in therapy. Almost inevitably, events or circumstances that
appear to have been stressful can be recognized—although, as
mentioned, not always by the patient. Investigating and suggesting possible explanations of what is happening in terms of
its stressful nature can generally relieve anxiety, although
when onset took place a number of years previously, this process can occasionally reactivate anxiety. If this occurs, diversion from discussion of such stressful circumstances is generally advisable. Use can be made of anxiety management
techniques (including relaxation) and supportive psychotherapy.

Study 2: The Man and the Moon

William is a 40-year-old with a 22-year history of schizophrenia. During that time he has been admitted to numerous hospitals and prisons across the British Isles, causing much distress and many practical problems for his mother (who has,
however, continued ably to support him). He has a history of
drug and alcohol abuse in addition to this. His compliance
with medication has been erratic, and this has frequently precipitated admissions.

During one such admission, he was noted to have been
asked, "How is the world today?"; he responded, "It is still
spinning round with the sun there and the moon there." In
1989, he was admitted urgently to our unit at his own request
in a very agitated state because he was "frightened that the
moon would fall in on me." At the time the moon was large
and full in the sky, and it was possible to imagine that the
patient alone in his flat, looking up at it, might question why
if other things fall to earth (airplanes, meteors, etc.), the moon
should not do so as well. It was decided therefore to treat this
belief as originating from a lack of real-world knowledge. An
explanation of gravitational and rotational principles, based
on very elementary physics, was given. William accepted this,

and he can now look back with amusement at this particular belief.

In the years since, he was not presented with psychotic symptoms and has taken medication regularly. He was admitted briefly once, in 1990, after a disagreement with his mother when he became agitated but not psychotic. He continues to live in his flat, receiving regular visits from his mother and a community nurse. He also takes a low level of oral neuroleptic, his mother having decided that depot injections did not suit him.

Discussion: William had a long history of bizarre behavior and a very unsettled lifestyle. On this occasion, gentle inductive questioning in the context of a sound therapeutic relationship enabled the use of real-world knowledge to combat the bizarre delusion that he had developed. He had become very frightened by the implications (as he saw them) of his belief. The generation of an acceptable alternative explanation as to why the moon would not collapse onto the earth, at least not for a few hundred million years yet, relieved this anxiety and reduced his distress.

EXPLANATIONS

Providing an explanation of the symptoms of depression (Beck et al., 1979) or anxiety (Beck et al., 1985) to patients is fundamental to the application of cognitive therapies in these conditions. Similarly, explanations of schizophrenic symptoms seem to be necessary if we are to develop the use of cognitive therapies in schizophrenia. The following initial areas are worth selectively describing to patients.

Continua of Functioning

The evidence that symptoms in schizophrenia merge with "normal" behavior can be described. Delusions, overvalued ideas, and strongly held beliefs are intermediate points on a functional continuum. The same can be said for hallucinations, pseudohallucinations, illusions, and normal perception. In other words, it can be suggested that evidence points to the conclusion that the symptoms a patient is experiencing are different in degree from, or are exaggerations of, normal responses to stress; they are not distinctively different in type.

"Normal" Experience

The experimental evidence that similar, if not always identical, symptoms and signs occur in "normal" subjects can be discussed. Hallucinations and delusions can occur in organic confusional states such as those caused by severe infections (pneumonias, etc.) or hallucinogenic drugs (which are recognized as producing psychopathological phenomena indistinguishable from those in schizophrenia). They can also occur in solitary confinement, in hostage situations, and in sleep and sensory deprivation experiments. In the extremely common situation where patients have been sleeping poorly or not at all, an explanation that this is a possible factor in their illness and one that is correctable can be very reassuring.

Cultural Beliefs

Delusional beliefs and passivity phenomena can be related to commonly occurring cultural beliefs. Thought broadcasting and insertion have culturally (even if not scientifically) acceptable equivalents in beliefs in telepathy. Similarly, delusions of control by external forces closely resemble beliefs in supernatural phenomena (e.g., poltergeists), astrology, religious and magical forces, and hypnotism. Such beliefs can be described as scientifically disputable, but they are held by many members of our society.

The experimental evidence about telepathic communication and other phenomena can be discussed. Essentially, the few reasonably well-controlled studies (see Tyrrell, 1960) that have investigated this suggest the possibility that names of colors, shapes, or playing cards can be "picked up" more often than would be expected by chance. However, there is no evidence that transmission of complex thoughts of the nature that patients describe can occur. Frank "scientific" discussion of this type appears to be appreciated by and influential with patients, even those of restricted educational background.

"Normal" Thoughts

Fleeting grandiose ideas, ideas of reference, and paranoid thoughts can be described as very common, perhaps even universal, in the normal population. For example, the belief that one would make a better prime minister or president than the present incumbent is a remarkably common grandiose idea. The experience of walking into a crowded room that falls silent as one enters can inspire ideas of reference ("What's wrong with me?"), and in certain circumstances the belief that everyone "is getting at me" when a series of events have gone against one is not uncommon. These beliefs occur spontaneously and are usually dismissed rapidly. However, at times of stress a "search for meaning"—a basic need to explain what is happening—can probably lead to more ready and lasting acceptance of such beliefs.

This may particularly be the case when an individual is isolated or feels unable to discuss such personal or intimate matters with parents (from whom he is separating and with whom relationships may have deteriorated) or with a partner or confidant (because close relationships outside the family have not been developed). Even in a case where communication can occur within such a relationship, at times the partner's or parents' beliefs or way of communicating them may be so abnormal as to confuse the patient further rather than enlighten him. Criticism of a destructive, all-embracing kind will tend to lead to further isolation and breakdown in communication, and has repeatedly been shown to be related to relapse.

Difference between Thoughts and Actions

It is important to stress the difference between thoughts and actions. The fact that persons think unacceptable sexual or aggressive thoughts does not mean that they have to act upon such thoughts. They retain the power of choice over their actions, even if thoughts come into their minds in an apparently uncontrollable way and even though they may feel out of control.

Vulnerability and Stress

A person's psychopathology needs to be explained in terms of the possible effects of stress on a vulnerable individual (i.e., the person himself). Vulnerability can be described to patients and relatives alike as including genetic and neuropsychological components; the latter are manifested by disorders of attention and processing of information. In a proportion of patients, this may be related to birth injury (or some developmental problem in late pregnancy) or other damage leading to ventricular enlargement but only becoming prominent after a period of maturation has occurred. It can also be explained that patients with schizophrenia seem to show abnormalities in their knowledge and understanding of everyday social issues, so that they may be more likely to develop culturally abnormal beliefs, and this may also be a component in the vulnerability.

However, it needs to be emphasized that most of those with these vulnerability characteristics, including many relatives, do not seem to develop the illness. Varying combinations of vulnerability characteristics with stressful events seem necessary for the illness to be precipitated, and also for it to persist or recur. Different components of these rationales need to be used selectively in attempts to explain specific symptoms as they are presented rather than being used as sweeping generalizations to cover all individuals.

In other words, the basic concept of a vulnerability–stress predisposition needs to be explained to most patients and relatives in terms such as the following:

> Stress seems to affect people in different ways, depending on their makeup. This includes any family susceptibility, personality, and possibly even brain structure. The same sort of stressful events may make some people depressed or anxious, but they may not affect others at all. In your circumstances, you have begun to . . .

The symptoms that have developed are then explored and discussed on an individual basis.

Study 3: Overwork and Vulnerability

John is a 25-year-old who lives with his parents and is quite shy and quiet. He attended "remedial" school as a child and had not had a permanent job until 2 weeks prior to psychiatric referral at the age of 22, when he started working nights at the factory where his father worked. Within days, he had developed the belief that a workmate was talking about him and accusing him of smelling. He started hearing voices commenting on his actions, and came to believe that people could read his thoughts and put thoughts into his mind. On presentation, he was retarded, very anxious, and sleeping poorly. His parents sought help for him, although he had little insight into his psychotic symptoms.

John's symptoms were explained to his parents and himself as possibly brought on by the pressure of a new, demanding job, and exacerbated by the sleep disturbance (caused by working on the night shift) and by his anxiety. His mother had already reached this conclusion. John accepted this explanation, as well as the explanation that medication was being prescribed "to assist your sleep and ease the confused, muddled thoughts and sensations, such as the voices, that you are experiencing." He was not admitted to the hospital but was supervised by a community nurse at home. He returned 5 days later much improved, with the voices and thought disorder now absent.

However, a week later John's mother—who had herself been hospitalized many years previously with a diagnosis of schizophrenia—was again admitted to the hospital, although this time in an overactive and overtalkative state (subsequently diagnosed as hypomania). She took over 7 months to recover fully from this. Her son, in the meantime, stopped taking medication of his own accord, and a week after her admission he began to hallucinate again. His father came with him to the clinic and discussed his own feelings of guilt at pushing his son into taking the job at his factory. Both father and son recognized John's hallucinations as symptoms of his illness, and he readily restarted medication and accepted referral to a day hospital.

At this writing, John has not required hospitalization, but still occasionally hallucinates and asks for adjustment to his low level of medication when this occurs. He now attends a day center with a view toward eventually attempting to work again, and has developed a varied social life. He has demonstrated to staff members an encyclopedic knowledge of popular music. His mother has fully recovered.

ELICITING DISTORTED THOUGHTS

Our experience is that even markedly thought-disordered patients are frequently able to respond to gentle and specific questioning, although patience and an ability to rephrase questions are often necessary. The period prior to the development of symptoms should be concentrated on, although frequently prior events and relationships dating back many years seemed to be important in determining why distorted thoughts are of individual significance. With patients presenting for the first time, events and thoughts are generally easier to elicit. But even with those who have been ill for many years, their memories or those of their relatives or family doctors (and clinical records) are generally sufficient to elicit events and thoughts of significance. Patients' accounts are couched in terms of their own understanding of what has occurred (e.g., overwork, marital breakdown, conscription into the army— often several such events in combination). Although such rationalizations can be suspect, the fact that they are considered significant means they are worthy of consideration. More often than not, they do seem to turn out to be acceptable explanations.

Study 4: Ordering Thoughts in Thought Disorder

Bill, a 22-year-old single man, presented himself to our acute psychiatric ward in a floridly thought-disordered state, with prominent paranoid delusions and incongruity of affect. These symptoms had worsened over a 2-week period, during which time his sleep had become progressively disturbed. He had experienced two schizophrenic episodes during the previous 6 years, which were treated with neuroleptics and cognitive therapy, and had returned to work on both occasions. No underlying organic disorder or history of drug abuse was detected.

Bill was admitted and treated with neuroleptics. Cognitive therapy sessions were included in his program. Rapport was established early, but progress was impeded by intermingling of themes and derailment, which at times lapsed into total incomprehensibility.

Bill gave informed consent (confirmed at a later stage) to the videotaping of an interview for teaching purposes. Review of this videotape demonstrated that four clear themes were present: references to a minor road traffic accident that he had witnessed; his mother's ill health; concern about somatic symptoms of anxiety, especially "breathing difficulties"; and finally intermittent references to the videotaping process itself as a form of "experimentation." In relation to this last theme, he referred to having half-Jewish parentage and later specifically mentioned experimentation. These specific fears were decatastrophized (see "Decatastrophization," below). After repeated reviewing of the tape, such references accounted for all areas that had previously appeared incomprehensible.

Subsequent sessions focused clearly on Bill's fears and on incorporating the sleep disturbance as a rationale to explain his symptoms. This may have contributed to his rapid improvement, allowing him to be sent on extended leave from the hospital within 3 weeks. After a brief recurrence of thought disorder, he was discharged to outpatient care symptom-free.

Discussion: Examining the themes of Bill's thought disorder seemed to assist the development of empathy and meaningful communication. Discussing these themes and tracing their antecedents helped to establish some of Bill's underlying fears. Subsequently focusing upon them, one at a time, and returning Bill to the theme being dealt with when he strayed, seemed to assist him in reordering his thoughts. His belief that the videotaping was an "experimental situation" needed decatastrophizing, but fortunately the rapport that had been developing, building on the previously established therapeutic relationship, greatly assisted in this.

DELUSIONS

The exploration of the events described as preceding or co-inciding with the onset of symptoms is used in unearthing the cognitions that preceded the acceptance of delusional ideas. This in turn will generally lead to the identification of faulty cognitions in the present, which usually relate to excessive self-reference. They are mediated via cognitive distortions— that is, personalization ("taking things personally"), selective abstraction ("getting things out of context"), and arbitrary inference ("jumping to conclusions"). These cognitions can also be detected by the patient in relation to symptomatology thought to be arising from the delusion—for example, the headaches and stomach pains attributed by Bernard to the satellite (see Study 1, above). The patient can then list his automatic thoughts and decide whether or not these are reasonable by examining the evidence. Very often, through "guided discovery" the patient will realize how unrealistic they are and how they relate to his emotions. Rational responses are then formed and used by the patient whenever such symptoms are noticed to be emerging. With these techniques the underlying schemata may gradually be weakened, as in Bernard's case. Other classical techniques can be used, such as reattribution and role play.

Tackling Delusions

When it is decided to tackle the delusion itself, this should be done when rapport is deemed sufficiently strong. Working from more superficial to deeper levels would seem most likely to be effective in working on delusional symptoms. However, many patients present the delusions that most distress them persistently, and with care discussion of these at an early stage is not necessarily contraindicated. They cannot and should not be tackled by direct confrontation, because the degree of emotional investment is usually too high. Such methods merely result in argument and worsening of symptomatology.

To discover underlying assumptive schemata, the technique of inference chaining (the "downward arrow" technique) can be used to discover the "hot" cognition—the one with most emotional investment. This essentially means following cognitions back to their origins in the cognitions coinciding with delusion emergence. The generation of alternative explanations and "Socratic questioning" (i.e., leading a person by logical disputation to a different conclusion from the one held) can then be used in attempts to modify such cognitions. The underlying schemata can be tackled using analysis of evidence, disputation, and behavioral experiments, as described by Ellis (1962). These schemata may represent distortions of classical ones (e.g., "Life should be fair," "I must be approved of") by repeatedly invalidating events. Alternatively, very negative schemata (e.g., "Nobody can be trusted," "I am unlovable") may have emerged through stressful circumstances.

These schemata may also present as delusional systems about the world—for example, that the patient is a victim of overwhelming forces over which he has no control, or that he has special powers or abilities that differentiate him from the rest of mankind. In cases where these beliefs are "silent," developing a rapport, using techniques for eliciting such assumptions in neurosis, and good psychiatric practice will enable them to be explored and debated.

Behavioral exercises or experiments including imagery (e.g., putting the person in an emotional situation in imagination, and showing him that he can change that emotion) may also be pertinent to the treatment of delusions. But they may be too powerful, and so need to be used with special caution. The patient should have low levels of anxiety, and a good therapist–patient relationship is essential.

Tactical Withdrawal

Attempts at direct confrontation of beliefs need to be strenuously avoided, as it is likely that this would almost certainly be ineffective, might be distressing, and possibly could even be dangerous. If discussing beliefs or delusions starts to increase distress significantly, it is safest to withdraw and make careful attempts at a later stage (often when medication has begun to take effect) to re-engage the patient in discussion.

Study 5: "I'll Be No More a Rover"

Jenny, now 58 years old, originally presented with symptoms of a depressive psychosis with paranoid features at the age of 35, in the context of marital disharmony. She continued work as a residential cleaner at an army cadet school until her husband's death by suicide when she was aged 39. She was seen psychiatrically soon after this, and on this occasion diagnostic features of paranoid schizophrenia were present.

Over the next 14 years Jenny worked intermittently, but eventually lost her home and traveled to Scotland, where she was born and raised and where some of her family still lived. She moved back and forth between Nottinghamshire (where her son continued to live) and Scotland over the next few years, living in various lodgings and sleeping rough. Her paranoid delusions persisted and worsened over this period. She believed she was under surveillance with regard to terrorist activities and "subject to the Official Secrets Act," with reports about her being sent to the Queen. She was eventually brought to the attention of our psychiatric services by the police. She discussed her psychotic complaints readily, and evidence was weighed with her in relation to them. She was garrulous and clearly had difficulty "taking the role of the other." Despite accepting that she needed help of an undefined sort, she refused admission to the hospital, and it was eventually decided that she should be compulsorily admitted.

However, once Jenny was told that she could be compelled to come into the hospital, she came readily and stayed without difficulty. After the initial discussions of her delusions, they were not probed further, as attempts at rational discussion led to her becoming increasingly garrulous and agitated. Gradually, during her rehabilitation period on a hospital hostel, she discontinued voicing the delusions. It is of course unlikely that they have disappeared wholly, but her behavior has moderated to such an extent that she is now living independently in her own council flat (i.e., apartment in public housing). We decided initially to attempt not to use medication, because we were concerned about it as a source of further conflict, as well as about likely problems with long-term compliance. It has not been necessary, as yet, to commence it.

Discussion: Jenny presented to our services after becoming homeless as a consequence of her illness. Her delusional system was not amenable to direct therapeutic intervention, and tactical withdrawal was the only possible response. Nevertheless, relations were subsequently developed with her and she has accepted a rehabilitation program that has (thus far) been successful in allowing her to regain an independent but secure existence.

"Agreement to Differ"

"Agreement to differ" is an essential tactic used to avoid prolonged repetitive discussion. It does not confirm the delusional beliefs; it assists in termination of discussions; and, where necessary, it enables a therapist to propose detention or compulsory admission to a hospital (in Britain, under the relevant section of the Mental Health Act) in as amicable a way as possible. The ideas discussed at this stage will have time to germinate and we have found that patients frequently return to them at a later date. When symptoms do not rapidly remit, it is often still possible for patients to accept that what seemed to be originating from outside themselves exists only in their minds and is a result of the illness that is called schizophrenia.

Delusional Perceptions

"Delusional perceptions," i.e. private meanings attached to consensually validated phenomena, occur in cases where a real event or occurrence (e.g., a traffic light changing from red to green) is endowed with a significance that seems quite inappropriate (e.g., that God has descended from heaven). Generally, preceding the emergence of such delusional perceptions, the person has been becoming progressively more anxious and confused (i.e., a "delusional mood" has been developing) and may have been experiencing overt psychotic symptoms (e.g., "voices"). He seems to be searching for explanations for the distressing feelings that he is experiencing, and in this highly stressed and consequently suggestible state he applies significance for the flimsiest reasons. For example, "Green means go; go is short for God; therefore God has descended from heaven" is a possible sequence.

The acceptance of such an explanation can paradoxically be markedly anxiety-relieving, so that it reinforces acceptance of the belief. Further examination of the belief can easily reactivate the previously felt dysphoria; this effectively discourages such deliberation. In discussion of such beliefs, it is therefore very important to monitor the level of distress that the patient is feeling and generally to keep it at a low level, as rapport may be lost easily. It is very tempting at times to try to break through the delusion by forceful and repetitive statements or advice. This is wholly counter-productive, in our experience, and can irremediably damage the therapeutic relationship.

Working with delusional perceptions involves first tracing the sequence back to where the initial unpleasant feelings commenced, and then proceeding through the increase in intensity to the moment when significance was applied to the specific occurrence. Therapy proceeds by analyzing this moment in a logical fashion and supplying alternative explanations. The therapist will generally discuss the impact of stress on the person and the resultant effect on suggestibility, as in this example:

Perhaps you thought [the perception] was significant because you were feeling quite worried and confused because of all the strain at work. When people are under pressures like that, sometimes they can read significance into situations inappropriately.

The analogy of "brainwashing" techniques can be useful in persuading patients of the way stressful circumstances can be used to influence people. The initial intention is to sow a seed of doubt in the delusional conviction. Brief, "matter-of-fact" explanations seem more effective than lengthy debates. "Agreement to differ" again may be an essential tactic.

Study 6: "I'm 150 Years Old"

Cecily, now aged 77, was admitted to a mental hospital in 1949. She remained there until she was transferred to a hospital hostel in her district of origin in 1986. At that stage she expressed the belief that she was 150 years old, yet constantly carried a teddy bear around with her.

Although Cecily's belief and bizarre behavior did not seem of great practical importance, such statements and behavior meant that others (including her close family) ostracized her. It seemed worth tentative discussion, therefore. Her therapist showed her medical notes to her; these demonstrated that her age was 70, and reinforced that as far as anyone knew, this was indeed her age. She referred to this investigation a number of months later when asked her age, and responded appropriately.

However, 2 years later she believed her age had advanced to 73, and a similar method was used to re-establish her actual age. The teddy bear was replaced in her affections by a dog bought for the hostel. The teddy bear was left in her bedroom, on the agreed basis that this was more socially appropriate at her age. She nevertheless continued to buy clothes for it and talk to it.

We were concerned that the targets chosen should not cause Cecily undue short-term distress, even if improving her social acceptability could be expected in the long term to improve her quality of life. Such short-term distress does not appear to have occurred. She has now re-established some family contacts and visits a local luncheon club regularly from the hostel. She is independent within the hospital hostel, and we would anticipate that she could survive well in less supported settings. However, she has expressed a clear desire not to move, and this has been respected.

Discussion: Cecily's case illustrates the use of hypothesis testing: Evidence was gathered and examined with her in relation to her age disorientation. Alternatives that she could accept were also developed to reduce her bizarre behavior.

SPECIFIC DELUSIONAL CONTENT

Study 7: The Chinese Connection

Ronald, a 54-year-old single man, was admitted to the hospital under Section 3 of the Mental Health Act. He complained of 20 years of systematic persecution by a group of Chinese gangsters called the Triads (which had been developed as a delusional perception). He had even decided to stab his 83-year-old neighbor, whom he believed to be a conspirator. He said that he had suffered enough and intended to travel to London to throw himself off the Post Office Tower. Emotional blunting, reduced self-care, and reduced drive were also present. He had been admitted on four occasions previously, but had always refused neuroleptic or other treatment. He lived alone in a run-down inner-city area.

Ronald was very eager to talk about his persecution and engaged well in therapy. The technique of peripheral questioning was used with reality testing, to tackle the central delusion of persecution by the Triads. He and his therapist agreed that he would go out to look for evidence of his delusions and record these in a diary. He was amazed to find that he returned with a blank sheet of paper. His rating of belief intensity fell from 100% to 20% within six sessions, and the alternative belief that his mind might be playing tricks on him (because of isolation, lack of sleep, etc.) rose from 0% to 80%. He then agreed to start taking sulpiride (200 mg three times a day).

As the delusion was given up, Ronald became markedly depressed; however, as he continued with schema-focused cognitive therapy, his affect gradually improved. His predominant schema emerged as a need to be appreciated as special. Once this was understood and discussed, there was considerable expression of appropriate emotion, as he had previously perceived rejection by his mother. Therapy then focused on a reduction in his demand to be seen as special and a reorientation toward a true assessment of the family situation. The content and form of the delusion therefore became understandable, in relation to this schema and the fact that some prisoners of war from the Far East had been kept on his family's farm during World War II. Ronald's self-esteem rose and his depression lessened, and there was a consequent sustained improvement in negative symptoms, with better self-care and a widening of social interests. He remained well at a 6-month follow-up.

Discussion: Ronald's case illustrates the important elements of a cognitive therapy approach to a delusion. Engaging with the patient and building rapport were initial "rate-limiting steps" and were characterized by empathy and collaborative empiricism. There followed the creation of an explanatory model of symptom emergence and maintenance, which addressed both the processes and content of the experience. The antecedents of delusion emergence were examined by means of inductive questioning. Treatment of the delusion then proceeded through peripheral questioning (in a non-confrontational, noncolluding way) and graded reality testing. Ronald's emotional investment in his delusion was reduced so as to lay it bare for these techniques. The schema underlying the delusion was detected from the general themes in the automatic thoughts and through the use of inference chaining, which revealed painful repressed emotional material.

Reference

Ideas and delusions of reference may relate to radio or television programs or to other people. Discussion should elicit which programs or circumstances are associated; news programs are particularly common (Smyth, 1990). It should then focus on what was said that the patient considered to relate to him. Alternatives can then be discussed. A homework task—to note when such references seem to occur over the period between sessions—can be set if the patient is uncertain, says that all programs cause such problems, or seems to become agitated when remembering specific details. Further tasks may be to listen or watch programs that cause such problems (once these are identified), so that the patient can desensitize himself to these references. Such attention to detail is often therapeutic in itself; the patient frequently returns rather surprised at the lack of occurrences over the period studied.

An occasional complicating factor that may arise is that "voices" referring to a patient come from the TV or radio. However, careful verbatim examination should distinguish these from ideas or delusions of reference. Patients may hear speech or laughter from outside the room in which they are, and, in a sensitive frame of mind, may refer it to themselves. For example, one patient was sitting with a therapist in a windowless room when he overheard the comment (which was also heard by the therapist), "What a ripoff!", from outside the door. He referred it to himself, but accepted the explanation that the person who had uttered the statement was discussing a new carpet bought cheaply for the ward, which indeed seemed to be a "ripoff" (i.e., poor value). Again, therapist and patient need to analyze the specific statements made and to discuss alternatives.

Persecution

Delusions of reference are frequently persecutory in nature or develop into such. Tracing and weighing evidence are necessary. This should include a determination of motivation. For example, the therapist may inquire, "Why should your friends turn against you? Have you done anything to upset them?", or may gently pose a series of questions:

> Why would the government be sending agents to follow you? . . . Have you done anything seriously wrong? . . . Doesn't the government only send agents if someone is a

threat to national security or a criminal? . . . You are neither of those, are you?

Persecutory delusions may not be readily voiced, particularly if the therapist or the mental health service is included in them. Development of a good rapport seems to assist in allowing disclosure over time.

Study 8: "Thoroughly Schizophrenic"

Norman, now 56 years old, was described by a psychiatrist when he was 22 as "thoroughly schizophrenic, and the prognosis I would regard as hopeless." Both his parents had been admitted to mental hospitals with mental illnesses that would appear to have been schizophrenic in nature; his father spent a period in Rampton Special Hospital. Norman himself has had multiple and lengthy hospital admissions with paranoid schizophrenia.

Since 1984, Norman has had three periods of illness when danger to others has necessitated his transfer to secure accommodation for brief periods. On these occasions, his talk and behavior were violent and particularly related to concerns about "Japanese or Asian hordes invading and killing all," and he would become markedly thought-disordered. The development of these episodes and the content of his delusions seemed related to world news at the time. However, logical and reassuring discussion of these fears and generation of alternatives proved over time to be very useful tactics, in reducing his hostility, even when, as occurred on the first occasion, his hand was around the therapist's throat.

Since Norman's last discharge to his home, in 1992, he has continued to accept medication readily and to work each day in a voluntary capacity with a local builder. He has become progressively less thought-disordered and paranoid, to the extent that he does not at present display psychotic signs or symptoms. Prior to his last admission, when he was interviewed by a local newspaper with other members of a voluntary self-help group, the National Schizophrenia Fellowship, he talked lucidly about his illness and how it has affected him.

Discussion: Norman has presented very serious problems to psychiatric services over the years, and management of his aggressive behavior has been very difficult. When he has presented in an emergency, use of medication and reduction of danger to those around him have been the top priorities. However, even (perhaps especially) in these fraught circumstances, discussion of his fears and their antecedents and the generation of alternative explanations have assisted in calming him and limiting damage. He has now developed considerable insight into his illness, which we sincerely hope will be of benefit to him in the future. It has also been of assistance in improving his compliance with outpatient care and medication, both of which he now accepts readily. Recently he survived without relapse his transfer from depot injections, because of problems with his injection sites, to oral medication.

Grandeur

Perhaps more than other delusions, those of grandeur can prove difficult to deal with by cognitive means, because of their reinforcement by the elated mood that generally accompanies them. In other words, patients with grandiose delusions feel good rather than anxious or frightened, and a major motivating factor in resolution (i.e., relief of the unpleasant feelings that accompany persecutory ideas) is not available. The effect of the grandiosity is predominantly felt by others, and paranoid elaboration can develop readily into lack of acceptance by others of grandiose beliefs.

Grandiosity has also been demonstrated to be associated with drug noncompliance (see "Specific Problems with Medication Compliance," below). Reasoning techniques may nevertheless sow doubt and reduce the expression of the grandiosity. For example, the therapist may say:

> I know you believe you are a special messenger from God, but unfortunately nobody else, not even your family, seems to agree. . . . Do you think in those circumstances it might be better to keep it to yourself, or at least just discuss this with me, and get on with your life? . . . You

have tried to persuade others. Maybe you and they are just going to have to wait and see.

The function of the delusion in the person's life can be tackled and often it is worthwhile to engage the patient in inference chaining at an early stage.

Study 9: The Mistaken Inventor

Ian, now 49 years old, developed paranoid schizophrenia with prominent grandiose delusions in 1985. He believed he had invented a "radio," which he later decided was the videocassette recorder. This idea, he claimed, was stolen from him by a television company after he sent details of it to a political interviewer. He believed he was not being allowed to develop it because he was "working-class." He also developed the belief that Princess Diana (who was actually coming at that time to visit the unit and officially open the hospital) was going to give him a uniform with his "coat of arms," confirming his belief that he was descended from royalty. It then emerged from his wife, who has since divorced him, that he had traced his descent (with the help of a relative) to a duke, and that his problems developed from then on—particularly ideas of reference.

Ian recovered from the first episode of his illness, but did not comply with medication. He relapsed after 2 years, and cognitive therapy was then introduced for the first time. The evidence for his beliefs was weighed with him exhaustively during the early stages of therapy, as it appeared that he had elaborated ideas that had a kernel of truth into grandiose delusions. He seemed to have developed a paranoid reaction to others because of their failure to recognize his grandiose view of himself. He continued to hold his office job for a number of years, but was eventually laid off. He began predicting that the end of the world would occur when Halley's Comet arrived, and has repeated similar predictions since.

In 1988, he had to leave his home because of being unable to pay his mortgage, and he spontaneously left the district despite the offer of sheltered accommodation. Six months later he presented himself at our psychiatric unit and agreed to admission "overnight," although he still asserted that he was not ill. He had been traveling the country looking for the factory producing "his" videocassette recorders.

After 6 months he was offered a flat by the local housing authority, but turned it down because he was "expecting" a large sum of money in the post. At the time of this writing he now lives in a Social Services hostel, still very deluded but cooperative. Medication, when he has agreed to take it, has not made a noticeable difference in his delusional symptoms. He assists with domestic chores and is reasonably well settled. He and his therapist have "agreed to differ" about his delusional ideas. He seems to be beginning to voice them less frequently. He does not appear to have developed marked negative symptoms, in that he remains emotionally expressive and quite well motivated.

Discussion: Ian remains very disabled by his delusions, but seems much less distressed by them. They seriously affect his ability to relate to others. Tracing the antecedents of the delusion has led to an understanding of it, but neither this nor the generation of alternatives has proved successful in modifying it. The process may, however, have assisted in the development of rapport; it is noteworthy that he returned to the unit when he had nowhere else to go. Agreement to differ has been necessary, as discussion reached a stage where it was simply increasing his agitation.

Sexual Concerns

Sexual concerns are extremely common, although delusions of sexual change as such are not. The origins of such ideas may be similar, however; commonly, these involve adolescent insecurities about sex and guilt about masturbation. For example, one of our patients believed that his eyes looked different and that others could detect this because he had masturbated 14 years previously while watching a neighbor in her house.

These beliefs may be reinforced by the side effects of

medication on sexual function, particularly when adequate explanations are not given or are not understood or remembered by the patient (see "Side Effects," below). Concern about reducing compliance may seem at times to mitigate against frank discussion; however, our experience is that compliance is markedly improved following such discussions and the use of patient information leaflets.

Religious Significance

Commonly occurring events such as religious festivals, symbols such as crosses, phenomena such as bright "blinding" lights, and even aspects of personal appearance such as beards and long hair can be imbued with religious significance, and "personalization" and arbitrary inferences can occur. Tracing back evidence (when appropriate, with religious advisors) can assist in reassessment and can change delusional convictions, (e.g., "I am Jesus Christ") to less fixed "as if" or "just like" phenomena (e.g., "Maybe I'm a bit like Jesus; I'm very sensitive, like him; I even look something like the pictures in the Bible of him"), which are increasingly amenable to reason.

Study 10: Religious Significance and Strange Associations

Frank, aged 31, lives with his elderly father, who has been psychotically depressed on many occasions; he remains obsessively concerned about his father. Frank presented initially because of his doctor's concern that he was depressed and dependent on benzodiazepines. He discontinued these while attending a psychiatric day center.

Two months after this, Frank developed religious delusions, including the belief that he was divine. He readily discussed these beliefs. The evidence he marshalled to support this hypothesis included citations from the Bible, which he believed referred to him because of his surname. The connection explained was extremely tenuous. However, alternative explanations and the suggestion that he discuss his beliefs with the hospital chaplain assisted in his eventually rejecting these beliefs.

He then started to discuss a complex theory relating religious symbolism to bowels and specifically to feces. Exploration of this traced the origins of the theory back to photographs of religious architecture that he had seen in a library book. Frank agreed to bring the book to the next treatment session, and we examined the specific photographs involved. They contained cylindrical objects in dark black-and-white backgrounds. It was possible to appreciate the "fecal" resemblance, but also to discuss the much more likely alternative explanations. This seemed to satisfy him, and he stopped making references to the theory. He then looked into other religions, including Hinduism, through research in his local library, but eventually became less obsessive about the theme. He remains interested in religion, but in a seemingly appropriate way.

On one occasion, after an argument with his father (who was becoming particularly possessive), Frank left home. When he reached Euston Station in London, he believed he heard over the loudspeaker, "South Africa has hot baths for you." Exploration of this with him led to his conclusion that in the context of his ambivalent feelings about leaving home, South Africa symbolized a new, fresh start. The likelihood of his having misheard what was said, and falsely attributing it to himself while in a distressed state, was agreed to be a possibility. Later, after returning home, Frank saw a small parakeet in his garden, which he interpreted as associated with South Africa and his previous experience. He explained that he made this association because he had seen a television program about South Africa that had flocks of parakeets in it. More probable alternative explanations were again discussed and tentatively accepted.

Since 1987, when Frank first presented psychotic symptoms, he has had just two brief episodes of hospitalization, despite his reluctance to take medication. He has however continued to attend therapy—at first once a month, and now once every 3 months as an outpatient—to discuss his beliefs and other concerns. He is presently symptom-free and is now considering taking up work opportunities. However, he has stereotypes of managers as always unsympathetic and work as always unstimulating and unrewarding. These overgeneralizations are currently being debated.

Discussion: The work with Frank illustrates the approaches that can be taken to delusional perceptions and religious delusions. Essentially, these involved inductive questioning tracing the antecedents of his beliefs, which took the form of overgeneralizations and arbitrary inferences. This was repeated with each new belief and was not unduly time-consuming. It assisted in rapport formation and maintenance.

PASSIVITY

"Made Feelings"

The assessment of "made feelings" and other passivity phenomena can be assisted by attempting to understand and help the patient understand them in terms of somatic symptoms of anxiety, as they generally appear to derive from that source. Alternatively, a physical illness can be misinterpreted in this way. For example, a patient described "archangels pulling at the back of my neck," which appeared to be a reference to tension in that position. "Electric shocks" or "creatures running up and down my skin" can be related to paresthesia (the "tingling" associated with hyperventilation).

"Made Thoughts"

Sexual and violent thoughts can be considered so repugnant that they are felt to be ego-alien. In other words, "These thoughts are so disgusting that my mind could not produce them; it must be controlled by someone or something else." Discussion needs to center on the variety of "normal" thoughts and the impossibility, according to scientific evidence, that such control can take place.

"Made Actions"

The dissociation that occurs with "made actions" can be analyzed, and possible underlying motivations can be discussed. There may be a logical or even delusional explanation for the actions. For example, a patient rushed round to his neighbors' front door and broke it down without explanation, and was convinced that he was "made" to do this; this could have been related to his beliefs that they were influencing his thoughts and keeping him from sleeping at night.

Study 11: Out of Control

Andrew, aged 19, presented as an emergency with voices talking about him (hallucinations in the third person) and delusions of control after his parents' marriage had broken up. He had felt torn between his mother and father, and this had been reinforced by their attitudes toward, and expectations of, him. He realized that he was under pressure and retained sufficient insight to express the fear that he was "going mad." He had been sleeping poorly, and so an analogy with sleep deprivation effects was used to provide a rationale for his experiences and for the use of medication. It was suggested to him that with the stresses that he had experienced and the lack of significant amounts of sleep, it was hardly surprising that he was feeling confused and distressed. In these circumstances and similar experimental ones, the therapist told him, hallucinations are not infrequent. The way the "voices" were talking about him, and the feelings of being controlled from outside, also seemed to be understandable in the context of the breakup of his family around him. He accepted medication to help him sleep and reduce the confusion he was feeling. He has not required hospitalization and is now symptom-free.

Discussion: Andrew's therapy illustrates approaches to hallucinations in the third person. Also establishing the context for the delusions of control assisted in a more appropriate interpretation of his situation. The use of information about sleep deprivation had a decatastrophizing effect and greatly assisted in his compliance with medication. It was also useful in altering his parents' attitude toward him.

THOUGHT INTERFERENCE

The relatively common belief that the patient's thoughts are being read or are shared with others can be discussed in relation to "telepathic communication" and the explanations previously described. The possibility that the patient does not understand the ability of others to perceive his nonverbal communication needs exploration, and general social skills education can be valuable. Like "made thoughts," thought insertion may relate to sexual or violent thoughts that are considered so repugnant that they are felt to be ego-alien. Discussion again needs to focus on the variety of "normal" thoughts and the essential difference between thinking something and doing it. Essentially, the person can choose how to act and behave in relation to thoughts generated spontaneously.

HALLUCINATIONS

Explanations for Hallucinations

Hallucinations are explained as phenomena that, although within the patient's own mind, seem to come from outside. It is essential for the therapist to convey to the patient that "voices" can indeed have the clarity of speech: "Do your 'voices' sound clear, like my voice speaking to you now?" Sometimes they are more indistinct and at times difficult to describe ("noises, thumpings"). They can be described as occurring in "normal" people ("you or I") who are subjected to specific or excessive stress. Sleep deprivation is of particular relevance, as many patients experience nights without sleep or with poor sleep in the period before psychotic symptoms emerge, and sleep disturbance and psychosis ratings have been demonstrated to be closely correlated. This evidence can be mentioned to the patient.

It is stressed that the fact that the patient is experiencing hallucinations does not mean that he is "mad," although we tend to use terms such as "out of touch." Insanity or psychosis is explained as more complex by definition, and it is fundamental that insight be lost. Just because the "voice" (or other perception) appears to come from outside the patient's mind, this does not mean that he inevitably has to accept that it is originating from there.

Reality Testing

It needs to be established in collaboration with testing the patient that if a voice comes from a source external to the patient, other people than the patient himself should be able to hear it. The patient should be asked to test this initial hypothesis by telling the interviewer whether he can hear the voice while they are together. If the voice is heard only when the patient is with his family or a close friend, similar testing can be suggested. Inevitably, unless the diagnosis is wrong (e.g., delusions of reference are being confused with "voices"), the interviewer, family members, or friend will be unable to hear the voice. Frequently such reality testing seems unnecessary, as the patient is aware that only he hears the voice; however, it is almost always therapeutic for the patient to test this out systematically with trusted others (see Figure 8.1).

Alternative explanations for the phenomenon are then developed. These may include the following:

1. The patient is being lied to.
2. The voice is being directed specifically at the patient so that others cannot hear it.
3. It is coming from within his mind (and, possibly, related to the stress that he is experiencing).

The arguments for and against each proposition can then be weighed. Sometimes patients find the second explanation acceptable, and it is then necessary to discuss how this could occur—and to present the scientific evidence that no such method of directing thoughts is known to exist. It is only rarely found that the voice only occurs when the patient is alone and again alternative explanations for this can be given.

It is often useful to treat hallucinatory themes as classical automatic thoughts using the techniques described by Beck and colleagues (1979, 1985, 1990). The percentage of belief in the content of the hallucination can be recorded, and then generation of rational responses can be pursued collaboratively with the patient. Typical themes include control, violence, identity, and sexuality, and often patients accept the content of the hallucinations without question. Use of rational responses (particularly on audiotape) can help to reduce the percentage of belief, as well as intensity and frequency.

At times patients appear to be describing obsessional thoughts as "voices." Some patients appear to move from one type of psychopathology to another, with improvement occurring along a line from "voices" to obsessional thoughts to unpleasant but resistible thoughts. Similarity with the vivid imagery that occurs after an emotionally disturbing event— for example, a road traffic accident, an LSD "trip," or even seeing a horror movie—can be discussed. Flashbacks from such events may have some bearing on the persistence of hallucinations.

Many patients describe the fear they experience in association with the first time they hallucinate and the period thereafter, which may include compulsory admission and be extremely traumatic. It is possible, though certainly unproven, that this fear imprints experiences in such a way that they become more likely to persist. Our experience is that rapidly reducing such fear at an early stage, by providing an acceptable explanation and using the other techniques described, seems to reduce the persistence and recurrence of hallucinations.

Study 12: "It's Just My Schizophrenia Playing Up"

Gwen, now aged 52, was admitted to hospital on two occasions in 1985, within a year of the onset of her paranoid schizophrenia. Her husband had recently had a myocardial infarction and been hospitalized, being quite isolated in a small village, she became worried about living alone without him. She required compulsory admission to the hospital; however, she insisted that this was not just illegal, but (as she neologized it) "unillegal." Her delusional symptoms remitted, but she has continued to hallucinate intermittently, despite taking regular medication.

The reality-testing methods described above were used to help Gwen understand the nature of hallucinations. The evidence about the possible effects of stress and sensory deprivation was presented to reduce her fear. She now accepts that the "voices" come from within her mind and are caused by an illness, schizophrenia. Information about schizophrenia was given to her and her husband, with a particular emphasis on how well recognized an illness it is and how variable its course can be.

The "voices" now cause Gwen much less distress and are now rarely abusive to her. Her paranoid symptoms abated with the development of constructive therapeutic relationships with staff members, the therapist, and other patients. By the use of detailed recall, she found that her voices only occurred when she was alone, and she has found great benefit from attending and assisting at local day centers. The hallucinations now occur in the evening and at weekends, and although she would certainly prefer to be totally rid of them, she copes with her husband's support. When she hears them, she can now say, "It's just my schizophrenia playing up."

Discussion: Gwen's progress illustrates the use of reality testing of hallucinations, decatastrophization, and coping skills. The formation of a good rapport with her assisted in the management and possibly the reduction of her paranoid symptoms.

IDENTITY

Questions about personal identity emerge frequently in younger patients—for example, "Who am I?" or "What is the purpose of being here?" Though such issues are by nature inconclusive and, without care, can become topics of protracted discussion, reasoning with the patient is useful in developing rapport and rational thinking strategies. Many authors have described a breakdown in ego boundaries as a fundamental deficit in schizophrenia. Clearly, the process of differentiation between what is internal (e.g., a thought) and what external, (e.g., a "voice" or a controlling force) is flawed, possibly as a result of some organic neuropsychological process.

The need of patients, especially (but not always) younger ones, to separate and stake out an independent identity is probably a major factor in the trauma experienced within families. In a case where a patient has directed his criticism toward the parents, we have sometimes accepted this as just if it is a manifestation of this striving for separateness. By "pushing away" the family through hostility and criticism, the patient may be able to define his reality boundary more clearly and may feel less overwhelmed. The closer the family relationships, the more likely this is to occur. Giving the family "permission" to allow separation, either geographically (allowing the patient to move to separate accommodation) or simply within the home (allowing the patient to spend increased time apart—e.g., alone in his bedroom), can reduce pressure and conflict. The therapist should reassure the family members that this separation is necessary and does not mean that they are not caring and concerned.

NEGATIVE SYMPTOMS

The problems engendered by low motivation and drive are probably the most daunting and frustrating to therapists. In this regard, these outweigh positive symptoms, which at least can usually be improved by medication. However, that same medication can easily have a detrimental effect, producing or exacerbating the negative symptoms. Although it is of course desirable to reduce positive symptoms to a minimum, total elimination of them is not essential if the cost is serious depression of drive. A small reduction in positive symptoms may be obtained at the expense of reduction in the drive to understand and cope with these symptoms and life in general, and may thus be seriously demoralizing.

Early Intervention

Prompt response to psychotic symptoms, or even the delusional mood preceding such symptoms, can in our experience assist in preventing the secondary effects of hospitalization, hastening discharge, and allowing patients to retain jobs and self-esteem. However, such a response involves a readiness to accept that a schizophrenic process may be developing. Although the use of frightening labels with patients should be avoided, a prompt reaction leads to appropriate interventions and reduces the family crises that so frequently accompany the onset of psychotic illnesses.

It does the patient no favors to send him away in the forlorn hope that his symptoms will remit without intervention. The attritional process of obtaining support at an early stage, about which relatives' organizations (e.g., the National Schizophrenia Fellowship in Britain) protest so vociferously, is unnecessary and profoundly damaging to family dynamics. We allow our fears of schizophrenia to produce a denial defense in ourselves, whereas even if firm diagnosis is not possible, monitoring of the situation and provision of a "lifeline" can be reassuring to distressed families and perhaps even prophylactic. There seems to be little if any evidence that revisiting, making a follow-up appointment, and/or suggesting that a family telephone a mental health team if the situation does not resolve within a defined period is in any way damaging. On the contrary, our experience is that such provision assists resolution of adolescent crises and facilitates rapid intervention if a psychotic illness does develop.

Long-Term Plans

In cases where negative symptoms have developed, they inevitably take time to resolve, and planning over a reasonable time scale (e.g., 5- to 10-year periods) is essential. The tendency to "push" rather than gently encourage is understandable, but is doomed to failure and demoralizing for both patients and therapists. The targets that are set need to be readily achievable and may require frequent readjustment. Activity scheduling can be useful, and mastery and pleasure charts can be used when a patient can cope with them, but the avoidance of failure is important for morale. Providing the patient with written information (leaflets, books, or even medical texts) about schizophrenia can also be surprisingly useful; we have yet to find that this creates increased distress or disturbance. Attentional and perceptual deficits manifested in concentration difficulties can be enormously frustrating. Slow, steady movement and consolidation of gains can lead to gradual progress, but may take years.

Fortuitous change is an important therapeutic factor. For example, a patient with marked depressive mood, abusive hallucinations, and absence of drive was maintained in his home through regular supportive contact over a 5-year period. He was making little progress and was at serious risk of suicide when his son and daughter suddenly started to see him regularly and take him to visit their homes, after years of not contacting him. This led to a dramatic improvement in his symptoms and personal appearance.

Allowing a patient to take the lead, even though he may only set unambitious targets, seems important. His ability to cope with the pressure of personal contacts may be very limited, and this may include the contact with the therapist. Infrequent but consistent contacts over a lengthy period may be more effective than short-term intensive work. Our inclination is to increase the amount of time we spend with patients when therapy is slow to progress; paradoxically, reducing contact may in these circumstances be more therapeutic. By using activity schedules with the help of staff members, the patient can come to see the balance between short- and long-range pleasures in his life. Very often, he needs to be able to see that he can make progress by working toward reasonable, achievable medium- and long-range goals.

Frequently, and again paradoxically, encouragement to do less even when the patient is doing very little can permit achievement at a very low level to occur and progress to begin.

COMMUNICATION

Nonverbal Communication

Perception of nonverbal communication has been repeatedly described as being abnormal in schizophrenia. It may therefore need to be discussed, as it appears that this abnormality may contribute to patients' belief that their thoughts or feelings are being read when they are simply being appreciated by others who have interpreted nonverbal cues. Social skills training may thus be considered useful, over and above its present, well-described position in rehabilitation programs.

Neologisms

The use of neologisms can markedly impair communication, but these generally appear to develop as hybridizations or condensations of recognized words. The meanings of such neologisms can be asked for, rather than being allowed to pass unremarked. Comments such as "I don't know that word; is it one of your own?", with further discussion and even the use of dictionaries, may help to impede the progress of neologisms into the patient's personal and potentially unintelligible vocabulary. One patient, for example, spoke of "decyanization," by which he meant that he believed there is a way by which people can disappear as if poisoned and dissolving.

Study 13: "Brain Waves" and "Hyperthought"

Kevin, aged 29, had been admitted in an acutely psychotic state three times over a period of 7 years. He was reluctant to take medication, and relapse was associated with his discontinuing it and with his use of cannabis. At such times, he developed the belief that a group of "superbeings" existed who could transmit thoughts "scientifically." On his third admission, in 1991, Kevin and his therapist agreed to discuss these beliefs further and do what they could to investigate them in a scientific manner. He suggested that just as voices can be transmitted through the air as sound waves, so might thoughts be transmitted as "brain waves." Analysis of this hypothesis with him led to agreement that this was an interesting theoretical possibility; however, it was not one recognized in practice. Also discussed was the rudimentary experimental evidence related to thought transmission as demonstrated by parapsychologists in the testing of telepathy. As noted earlier, this evidence suggests at best that names of colors, shapes, or playing cards can be transmitted more frequently than would be expected by chance, but there is no evidence that thoughts can be transmitted in the way Kevin described.

In conjunction with this, Kevin spoke of a belief in "hyperthought." The therapist pointed out that this is not a word recognized in the English language, but inquired whether he was trying to describe some sort of strange thoughts. Kevin explained that he thought his mind was full of more thoughts than other people's minds were. This was related to the way that his thoughts were racing when he became psychotic. This latter phenomenon was discussed with him, and he agreed that it might be related to his original belief. He also accepted that he might be better off avoiding the neologism, which would not be understood by others.

At the time of this writing, Kevin is working on a voluntary basis, is taking medication, and is symptom-free. He has survived the formation and breakup of his first significant relationship in many years. At times (particularly when he has been consuming alcohol), he recognizes that his thoughts are becoming psychotic, but he retains insight with the support of his mother and friends.

Discussion: Kevin's therapy illustrates the interception of neologisms, the use of reasoning processes with bizarre beliefs, and the introduction of evidence related to and disputing paranormal experience. It also demonstrates methods of early intervention and coping strategies with psychotic relapse. The reasoning approach seemed to improve Kevin's compliance with medication as well.

Metaphorical and Imprecise Speech

Language may be used in a metaphorical sense. For example, a patient spoke of his "lifeblood" being drained away, but he did not mean this in a literal sense (i.e., that blood was being removed from him); he simply felt lacking in energy. As frequently happens in "normal" speech, particularly under conditions of stress, words may be used imprecisely or even inappropriately. A patient can be asked to explain whether he means exactly what he has said, or plausible alternative explanations can be suggested to clarify complex statements. Attempts can be made to assist the patient in "taking the role of the other," which seems to be a central problem in language disturbance in schizophrenia. Patients seem to find it difficult to appreciate that they are not being understood. They may use expressions idiosyncratically without seeming to realize it. Simple role play and role reversal can help.

The Need for Accuracy

Accuracy and consistency are needed in statements to the patient. For example, if a patient states that a member of the KGB is trying to find him, one cannot reply with absolute certainty that this is not the case. Stating that it is extraordinarily unlikely under the circumstances is more pedantic but also more accurate. Careless, placatory answers may impair rapport, because they may undermine the patient's belief that his fears are being taken seriously. Family and staff members, including junior members of the nursing and clerical staff, can also be advised to avoid "humoring" the patient in a patronizing, placatory way.

HUMOR

The preceding statement does not mean that humor needs to be absent from all discussions with a patient; indeed, it can be a very valuable therapeutic tool. The distinction needs to be made between laughing at behaviors and statements in situations where the patient can be led to see their incongruity and even absurdity, which can be remarkably therapeutic, and laughing at the patient himself, which is wholly inappropriate. Humor can be tension-relieving for patients and therapists alike and can bring warmth to relationships. When used within a sound therapeutic setting in an appropriate way, it is relaxing and humanizing. We underestimate our patients' abilities (and this includes those with paranoia) to make the distinction described above.

Humor nevertheless does need to be used with caution and only in cases where a good rapport has developed. When patients do inappropriately feel that they are being laughed at, or simply feel that their beliefs are not being taken seriously, the style of cognitive therapy—involving regular checking of the patients responses to aspects of therapy—should allow this to be picked up quickly. This arbitrary inference can then be used therapeutically in looking at "oversensitivity." If such misinterpretations occur in therapy, they are also very likely to occur in everyday life or to represent patients' particular fears, and need to be discussed and explored.

ANXIETY MANAGEMENT

Many patients seem to benefit from learning a relaxation technique. Simply giving them a cassette tape of progressive muscular relaxation exercises, with discussion and then monitoring of its use, may be all that is necessary. The aim is to reduce the marked anxiety that many of the patients experience and that probably exacerbates their psychotic symptoms. It certainly increases their unease.

Hyperventilation has been described as precipitating hallucinations, and the use of relaxation has therefore a logical basis in these circumstances and can be carefully encouraged. Most of our patients who have been given relaxation instructions have been able to use them eventually, and most have reported general benefits. Some have reported specific improvement in psychotic symptoms and have used relaxation as a coping strategy. No patient has reported or been observed to experience negative reactions.

An explanation of anxiety symptoms needs to be given in cases where misinterpretation of such symptoms appears to be occurring. For example, the startle reflex and paraesthesia ("tingling" and numbness) resulting from hyperventilation appear at times to be misinterpreted as "electric shocks" being transmitted through the body or being touched by an invisible person.

One patient described a fear of going to bed at night because of "someone pressing on my chest." He therefore had slept on a settee in his living room for a number of months. A discussion of the probable cause of this sensation as hyperventilation leading to a feeling of overexpansion in his chest, and the use of a hypnotic, resolved this problem; the patient returned to sleeping normally in his bedroom.

HOMEWORK

Homework assignments can be used, but need to be appropriate to the patient's capabilities, for example, the therapist can suggest that religious voices or delusions be discussed with a hospital chaplain. Diaries of dysfunctional thoughts can sometimes be kept to identify thoughts occurring before or at the onset of psychotic symptoms. They can also be used to test abnormal beliefs and to study the frequency and pattern of symptoms. Generally, however, with our patients we have used detailed recall at the time of the interview of occasions when psychotic symptoms have occurred. The identification of situations in which specific stresses (e.g., being alone) provoked hallucinations or other symptoms has then been utilized in developing appropriate coping strategies.

COPING STRATEGIES

Strategies that patients themselves have developed to cope with their symptoms have been described over the past few years. These are extremely commonly used; few patients have not developed some simple way of alleviating at least some of their symptoms. Because there is evidence that some of these methods are useful to a variable degree in various individuals, we describe relevant ones to patients; we also encourage them to experiment and develop their own combinations of coping methods. Not only is this process educational, but it has symbolic significance in involving them even more closely in the management of their illness and reducing their feelings of powerlessness over it. It encourages them to develop methods of control and may even counteract passivity phenomena directly.

Five different groups of coping methods used by patients can be discussed with them:

1. *Behavior control*: switching on a radio, listening to music, increasing physical activity (e.g., going for a walk), decreasing physical activity (e.g., resting).
2. *Cognitive control*: use of redirection of attention—for example, attempts to ignore symptoms, distraction toward comforting ideas, problem solving by use of quizzes, or setting up a project.
3. *Socialization*: increasing social contact or avoiding it (although the latter appears surprisingly little used).
4. *Medical methods*: temporarily increasing oral medication or contacting a mental health professional.
5. *Symptomatic behaviors*: acting in some way in accordance with the symptoms (generally therapy is aimed at avoiding such responses, but in cases where these relieve distress without increasing social ostracism, they can be considered useful strategies occasionally and/or temporarily).

This list is by no means exhaustive, and individual assessment with patients is needed to determine which factors or strategies provide the most relief from their symptoms. They should be encouraged to use whichever strategies they find useful, providing these are not counterproductive in their long-term effects.

DECATASTROPHIZATION

Patients' Fears of "Going Mad" and Its Implications

The subjective fear of "going crazy" is one of the most frequent emergent symptoms of the onset of relapse, and probably of initial episodes; yet it is something rarely discussed with patients. Our impression is that the use of expressions such as "mad" or "crazy" is usually, although not always, inappropriate. "Losing touch," "going out of your mind," or "having a breakdown" can be substituted. Simply asking patients, "Are you afraid you are going out of your mind?" or the equivalent in the early stages of this process can open up discussion of a major fear.

When patients first start hearing voices, they often state, if asked, that they themselves think and fear that they must be "going mad." They also fear, with considerable and unfortunate justification, that if they say that they are hearing voices, others will also assume that they are "mad." These two fears may be accompanied by catastrophic cognitions of the probable implications, which include being taken to a doctor, who will make them see a psychiatrist. The patients may then be locked up forever in a "lunatic asylum," where they may be assaulted and terrorized by the "really mad" inmates. Such an anxiety feedback loop acts to increase the original distress and may hasten the emergence of psychotic symptoms (see Figure II.1). Paradoxically, the fear of "madness" may therefore be a significant factor in its development.

Families' Fears of Patients' "Madness"

Families frequently seem to catastrophize to at least as great an extent as the patients, developing fears of unpredictability, embarrassment, and violence. Decatastrophization in this case means discussing these fears with family members and breaking the feedback loop. The explanations of hallucinations discussed previously, and the relating of delusional ideas to cultural beliefs, can assist in this. A clear statement, such as "The fact that [your relative] is hearing voices doesn't mean that he

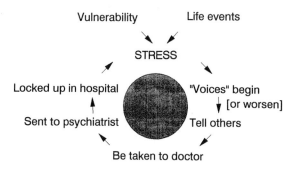

FIGURE II.1. The catastrophization cycle.

has lost touch with reality; the important thing is being aware that he is ill," can help relatives deal with these fears and reduce their criticism and hostility.

Families' Guilt

Work with families is an essential part of the management of schizophrenia, but the unfortunate legacy of early work—which blamed society and specifically parents for the illness—remains with us. The injustice of this is being increasingly recognized by mental health professionals, but it remains an essential issue to discuss with families.

We are not in a position to advise parents how not to have offspring who develop schizophrenia, or even how to reduce the risk significantly (apart from the very rare instances where genetic counseling is relevant). How then can they be blamed for this happening? They will inevitably blame themselves even without encouragement, and the argument we have just stated needs to be discussed with them to reduce such self-blame. They can, of course, still contribute positively to the recovery and maintenance of the patient by, for example, reducing critical comments and face-to-face contact. Again, of course, they may well themselves feel oversensitive and interpret such advice as criticism, and this in turn may need to be explored.

Fears of "Schizophrenia" as a Label

The diagnostic term "schizophrenia" can be extremely useful with patients and families in giving them a label, and with it at least the appreciation that "the doctor knows what is wrong." However, it often requires decatastrophization in its own right, because its use frequently precipitates fears of inevitable mental degeneration ("dementia praecox"), which may be interspersed with violent episodes, into a demented state. It is very important to deal with these fears and explain that our understanding of the outcome of the illness has considerably improved. We now recognize that many people with schizophrenia make a full recovery, and only very few spend their lives as permanent hospital inpatients. Recovery may be slow at times, but progress can occur over very lengthy periods.

The term is also very useful when a patient is relapsing into a psychotic state. Many of our patients, like Gwen (see Study 12, above), can now recognize the process by which this happens—"It's the old schizophrenia playing up again." They frequently use the term itself and other psychopathological terms, and can be reminded of the specific illness they are suffering from when they fail to recognize what is happening. Terms such as "hallucination," "delusion," and "thought interference" can be used similarly.

Biological explanations can be used, in cases where a therapeutic alliance has been forged, in discussions of what we do understand about the genetics and neuropathology of psychosis. This information can supplement the explanations of "internal" causes and vulnerability.

MEDICATION

As discussed previously, medication has proved of considerable benefit in reducing the severity and recurrence of the signs and symptoms of schizophrenia, and at times even in eradicating them. But many patients with significant disabilities in whom medication might be effective cannot be persuaded to take it at all or on a consistent basis because of (1) the very nature of the illness itself (e.g., the patients may not see themselves as having a "medical" problem or may have delusional beliefs associated with medication), and/or (2) associated concerns about medication (e.g., irrational assumptions about it, fears about side effects, or a lack of understanding about the purpose of taking medication).

Prescriber Considerations

Although the insight of the patient is a fundamental factor, it is also very important not to underestimate the complexity of the decision to prescribe medication. It is essential not to make inappropriate assumptions, and the following can usefully be reviewed:

1. Is the diagnosis secure?
2. Is short-term or long-term treatment intended?
3. How long a period is meant by "short-term" or "long-term"?
4. When long-term medication is appropriate, what characteristics of the individual's illness have contributed to this decision?
5. Why is this particular drug being considered?
6. Why this dose?
7. What side effects can be expected, in both the short and the long term?
8. What additional management (e.g., day care, befriending, support groups, community psychiatric nurse, outpatient visits) will be available?

Medication-Centered Cognitions

Prescription is a negotiation between the prescriber and the individual, and one in which evidence should be made available to answer the questions above in a form that can be understood but not catastrophized. The meaning of medication, the possible side effects, and any underlying assumptions need to be explored.

For example, a patient whose mother is severely disabled as the result of a neurological disorder (e.g., motor neuron disease) may misinterpret tardive dyskinesia (a side effect characterized by involuntary movements) as being of a similar nature. A patient who has read literature about antipsychotics that dramatizes their long-term effects may have an unbalanced understanding and may need to bring in the literature to discuss it. Or a person may have paranoid beliefs that he is being poisoned and may misinterpret the prescription of medication in this context.

An example of paranoid beliefs of this type was given by Satel and Sledge (1989); as described in Chapter 6, these authors used audiotape feedback and reality testing to correct beliefs in one patient that "her mother had hypnotized her as a child and given her medication that would cause her to be confused about her past" (p. 1013). Similarly, the onset of paranoid delusions can include such beliefs as "my colleagues were against me and they drugged my tea" (see Study 1, above).

Insight is variable, as described by David (1990) and reviewed earlier (see Chapter 11). It is not "all or nothing," nor is explicit acceptance of illness or the necessity for medication needed. The offer of medication even in the absence of insight can be surprisingly accepted.

Techniques of persuasion can be even more effective, and cognitive therapy of schizophrenia mobilizes these. Synergy between medication and cognitive therapy is a general feature of all the differing cognitive management programs being developed (Perris, 1988; Brenner, 1989; Kingdon & Turkington, 1991a), in contrast to psychodynamic approaches. The broad program used in destigmatizing and restructuring cognitions can be expected to assist with medication compliance, but specific elements can be focused directly on this area.

Rationale for the Use of Medication

Antipsychotic drugs are described as necessary to improve sleep and rest and to decrease "confusion" through their sedative effects, and to reduce hallucinations and delusions through less clear methods. The therapist can describe the rationale in terms such as these: "to assist your sleep and ease the confused, muddled thoughts and sensations, such as the voices, that you are experiencing." This can be elaborated by discussion of experimental evidence about sleep and sensory deprivation; in these states there is evidence that signs and symptoms similar (if not identical) to these of schizophrenia occur, and reference can be made to the work by Leff (1968) and Oswald (1974).

The evidence that lack of sleep and severity of psychotic disturbance are correlated (Meltzer et al., 1970), can also be described in supporting the use of medication. Sleep disturbance may be exacerbating the psychotic symptoms. When sleep has been erratic, suggesting that "whatever else is happening, you are clearly not sleeping properly and we need to help you rest, as it seems likely that lack of sleep worsens the problems you have" can be useful in effecting compliance with medication in acute situations.

Similarly, discussion of biochemical (especially dopaminergic) mechanisms of operation of medication (see Farde et al., 1988) can assist in explanation and compliance. The research data on the effectiveness of antipsychotics in treatment and prophylaxis may need to be reviewed in some detail; simply saying, "We know it works for some patients," will be insufficient. Depending on patients' level of intelligence or skepticism, and with their assent, photocopies of popular descriptions of drug mechanisms and of sleep and sensory deprivation (e.g., those in the book by Oswald, 1974) or even copies of the research studies themselves can be provided, with explanations.

Side Effects

Side effects need to be discussed frankly and appropriate warnings given whenever medication is commenced, however psychotic or reluctant the patient may be. In the latter case, the explanations will be briefer but, if anything, are even more necessary.

Misinterpretation of side effects is common, in our experience. Stiffness or intention tremor in association with parkinsonism can be interpreted as the patient's being controlled by external forces or, not unnaturally, being poisoned. Sedation may paradoxically cause anxiety and panic, and again may result in delusions of control. The "slowed-down" feeling may contribute to beliefs in thought interference. Delusions about sexuality (e.g., delusions of sexual change) may be reinforced by the occasional side effect of medication in reducing sexual function, particularly when explanations about these effects are not given or not understood or remembered by the patient.

When long-term medication is initially proposed to the patient, discussion of tardive dyskinesia at that stage (however briefly) is important in itself, not least because it reduces the chance of the patient's finding out about this side effect from other sources and feeling that the prescriber is in some way being less than truthful to him. The early warning signs that will be regularly checked for can be mentioned, so that if they should emerge, future medication use can be reviewed collaboratively.

Training in self-regulation of medication can empower the patient and thus can assist in improving compliance (Eckman et al., 1992).

Specific Problems with Medication Compliance

Some symptoms and signs present particular difficulties in relation to compliance:

1. *Grandiosity.* As described earlier (see Chapter 3), patients with grandiose symptoms were found in one study to be particularly noncompliant with medication and "seemed to prefer psychosis to normality" (Van Putten et al., 1976, p. 1443). Patients' choices may thus complicate the compliance and need to be taken into account. The grandiosity alone will not be sufficient reason for a patient's taking medication, but other symptoms (e.g., sleep disturbance or agitation) may be, and reasoning techniques may sow sufficient doubt to assist compliance and reduce the expression of the grandiosity.

2. *Negative symptoms.* Negative symptoms are generally not improved directly by medication; however, when positive

symptomatology is reduced, drive and motivation may improve. But that same medication can easily have a detrimental effect, producing or exacerbating negative symptoms. As noted earlier (see "Negative Symptoms," above), total elimination of positive symptoms is not essential if the cost is serious depression of drive. Therefore compliance, as well as negative symptoms, may paradoxically be improved by the therapist's tolerance of positive symptoms. Assessing in negotiation with the patient the significance of positive symptoms (e.g., hallucinations) in a person's life may lead to a reduction in medication and improved compliance, as occurred in the case of Gwen (see Study 12, above).

Structured reasoning, derived from cognitive therapy and using a research-based rationale for medication use and description of side effects, can assist in improving compliance with psychotropic medication (e.g., see Study 11, above). Cognitive therapy of schizophrenia aims in general to promote the appropriate use of medication, and the specific techniques described above may help therapists to correct faulty assumptions, educate patients, negotiate with patients, and reinforce the rational acceptance of medication. Explanatory and cognitive techniques may also reduce the amount of medication required for management of symptoms. It is possible that occasionally they have allowed successful treatment without medication; however, in the vast majority, psychotropic drugs remain absolutely essential. There is no indication that using cognitive techniques causes patients to be less likely to accept such treatments. Indeed, the contrary seems to be the case; that is, drug compliance is substantially improved. This in turn makes patients more accessible to therapy.

STRUCTURE OF SESSIONS

Sessions need to be conducted in a flexible manner, with their length and timing dependent on the patient's clinical state and progress. The initial assessment may take up to an hour; with more articulate, less distressed, or more garrulous patients it can take longer, whereas with agitated or retarded patients it may be considerably shorter. Initially, two sessions a week lasting between 15 minutes and an hour (averaging about 30 minutes) can be offered; these are tapered off rapidly to weekly and eventually monthly sessions.

Rarely, lengthy sessions are justified. For example, the exploration of a complex delusional system in one instance took 2½ hours; arbitrary curtailment of the session would have simply meant starting again on the next occasion and would have been upsetting to the patient, impairing rapport development. However, brief sessions over a period of months or, with those with established illness, even years seem to be most effective. We have incorporated such sessions into routine outpatient clinics.

Premature termination of sessions may occur when the patient (or, occasionally, the therapist) is tiring or becoming restless, or when all agenda items have been covered. Persistence when the former is recognized as occurring may well counteract any therapeutic work and damage rapport.

THE TREATMENT CONTEXT

The setting in which treatment occurs is important, although, at least in the short term, less-than-ideal circumstances may have to be tolerated. Multidisciplinary community mental health services with facilities available for day care, rehabilitation, and "asylum" are ideal but scarce. The concept of "normalization" is central to most such services now; however, its limitations need also to be accepted.

Admission of acutely ill patients to a hospital environment (even a district general hospital) is "abnormal" but frequently essential, if safe management and relief to the patient and those around him are to be offered. There is a clear need for "asylum" for the most vulnerable for short and extended periods, and again it is essential to be realistic about the time scale of therapy. Day care facilities, support groups, befrienders, and mental health staffs provide support and opportunities for patients to discuss and defuse their overvalued ideas, delusions, and hallucinations.

Early intervention before possible "hardening" of psychotic symptoms would seem to be critical, and rapid and easy access to the mental health staff of a service needs to be made available. Our use of "normalizing" rationales seems to have been facilitated by the provision of the "normalizing" environment that we have described earlier (see Chapter 13) and at least adequate resources.

THERAPISTS' NEED FOR SUPPORT

Our discussion of the use of these techniques has frequently given rise to speculation as to whether therapists using them may find it difficult to regain contact with reality themselves at the end of sessions. This fear is perhaps a factor in the relative neglect of the use of individual psychotherapy with schizophrenics. Certainly, using such techniques in isolation without the support and supervision of colleagues would be stressful, and therapists would become susceptible to demoralization, as is the case in all psychotherapeutic work. The limited experience of their use has not thus far suggested an increased proneness to psychosis in therapists, however.

OVERALL GOALS

The major goal set with all patients and their families is that of explaining and destigmatizing confusing and frightening experiences, while not losing sight of the fact that something is seriously wrong. The techniques described here also have great potential for mental health promotion, because they can provide explanations of phenomena that presently are misunderstood and frighten most people. Relating schizophrenia to normal experience can make it more accessible and can reduce societal stigmatization.

Medication and hospitalization are allies in therapy, with underuse being no less of an error than overuse. Overall, the development of a strong rapport with the patient and his relatives is of paramount importance. The serious discussion of confusing hallucinatory experiences and delusional ideas seems to be remarkably helpful in this.

The complete process of therapy as we envision it is illustrated in Figure II.2.

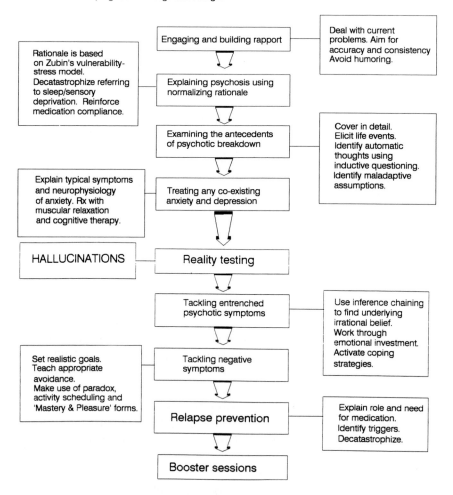

All patients have followed a flexible course of cognitive therapy with sessions of variable length.

Most have progressed through these stages:

Engaging and building rapport

Deal with current problems. Aim for accuracy and consistency Avoid humoring.

Rationale is based on Zubin's vulnerability-stress model. Decatastrophize referring to sleep/sensory deprivation. Reinforce medication compliance.

Explaining psychosis using normalizing rationale

Examining the antecedents of psychotic breakdown

Cover in detail. Elicit life events. Identify automatic thoughts using inductive questioning. Identify maladaptive assumptions.

Explain typical symptoms and neurophysiology of anxiety. Rx with muscular relaxation and cognitive therapy.

Treating any co-existing anxiety and depression

HALLUCINATIONS

Reality testing

Tackling entrenched psychotic symptoms

Use inference chaining to find underlying irrational belief. Work through emotional investment. Activate coping strategies.

Set realistic goals. Teach appropriate avoidance. Make use of paradox, activity scheduling and 'Mastery & Pleasure' forms.

Tackling negative symptoms

Relapse prevention

Explain role and need for medication. Identify triggers. Decatastrophize.

Booster sessions

FIGURE II.2. Process of therapy.

PART THREE

EVALUATION AND EVOLUTION

Schizophrenia can be such a distressing and disabling illness that when clinicians believe that those patients they are seeing are doing remarkably well, it is exciting and of course dangerous. Too many false dawns have been heralded in schizophrenia research, and caution must always be exercised until conclusive confirmation is obtained that benefit is accruing.

It may be that the excellent community psychiatric service in Bassetlaw is predominantly responsible for the improvements we think we are seeing. Drive and enthusiasm alone would not seem to be sufficient, but these factors could clearly be distorting our perception of improvement. They may be biasing the results we have seen although the absence of suicides, as yet, among the patients we are following is extremely encouraging in such a high-risk group.

Our next step, then, must be to evaluate effectively the techniques we have described. Psychotherapy demands such commitment from practitioners that such evaluation can be very difficult even to discuss in a detached and impartial manner. It feels at times as if such questioning is almost a personal affront. It is most difficult for it not to become personalized, and this is presumably in part why properly controlled trials in this area have been so infrequent in the past. Cognitive and behavior therapists, however, have demonstrated a readiness to apply such scientific techniques to their work over the past decade. It may also be that philosophical methods may assist in our appreciation of the concepts (such as "thought" and "delusion") that we use with so little consideration.

On the basis of our preliminary results, a pilot controlled study of these techniques has been designed and is underway. The initial intention was to test the feasibility of setting up a definitive study of these techniques. Our first major area of concern was that evaluation of psychotherapies under controlled conditions has so frequently proved controversial and difficult; the development and use of a placebo psychotherapy was therefore to be piloted-tested. Second, we recognized that the patient group is a difficult one to study under controlled conditions, because their problems are such that unpredictability and negativism may significantly interfere with the assessment and treatment processes. Finally, we decided that a small-scale study might demonstrate trends that would allow statistical power analyses to indicate how large a study will be necessary to have a reasonable chance of demonstrating statistical significance (if such exists).

The theoretical and methodological difficulties of placebo-controlled studies in psychotherapy research are well recognized. Parloff (1986) has discussed these in detail. Studies of psychotherapy have done the following:

1. Matched therapists who use different techniques of therapy (e.g., reality-adaptive supportive vs. exploratory insight-oriented therapy in the Boston Collaborative Study; Stanton et al., 1984).
2. Compared "active" treatments with placebo drug treatments (e.g., Tyrer et al., 1988).
3. Compared specific treatment and drug placebo groups with continuing "clinical management" by a team independent of the experimenters (e.g., Elkin et al., 1989).
4. Compared specific treatment and placebo psychotherapy, of which good examples in the literature are few.

The concept of a distinctively "placebo" psychotherapy has therefore been considered difficult. It might be taken to suggest that a relationship needs to be formed with a patient from which "therapeutic" benefits are excluded. Because this appears to be a practical impossibility, the concept of placebo psychotherapy would also appear theoretically impractical. However, placebos, such as those used in pharmacological trials, have been demonstrated to have beneficial effects on many occasions, and the fact that a placebo may be beneficial does not exclude its use. Placebos are included in most studies to control for suggestion and other so-called "nonspecific factors," and to assist in preserving the "blindness" of assessments by patients and experimenters.

Nonspecific factors that are common to various forms of psychotherapy have been identified by Frank (1973) and others. Truax and Carkhuff (1967) have identified characteristics in therapists that seem to coincide with patient improvement; they describe these as "accurate empathy," "nonpossessive warmth," and "genuineness." These are also probably the characteristics of a good friend, and are thus encouraged in the training of "befrienders" (Kingdon et al., 1989). In the context of a study of this nature, "genuineness" might seem impossible when researchers are testing a treatment that they have considerable commitment to and belief invested in, against a control therapy that they believe to be relatively ineffective. However, we still harbor some doubt as to whether the treatment will be effective under research conditions in comparison with the control treatment, and we accept that nonspecific factors can be sufficiently effective to permit the "genuine" use of a control treatment.

Moreover, to determine whether the techniques under investigation do more than simply provide a vehicle for well-meaning enthusiasm, the pilot-testing of a placebo psychotherapy seemed to be essential. This was therefore modeled on the concept of a hospital or community "befriender" who would encourage and listen to a patient, using nondirective techniques. It also seemed necessary to include some specifically medical intervention, as the patients (particularly those with pre-existing paranoid ideas) and their families might find it difficult to accept a doctor who did not discuss medical matters with them.

A standard description and explanation of schizophrenia was drawn up and circulated for comment to senior psychiatric colleagues, for validation of it as "traditional" and noncontroversial. This was then used in discussion with patients where appropriate. Consideration was given to the audio- or video-taping of sessions, to establish that differences could be detected between the two types of intervention. However, we were concerned that this might interfere with the delicate process of establishing and maintaining rapport with a group of patients in whom, as discussed previously, this is notoriously difficult and is a fundamental focus of the "active" treatment. We were also concerned that delusional elaboration related to the recording process and apparatus used might complicate matters, as described by Sacks and colleagues (1974) in their research with patients with schizophrenia.

There are clearly difficulties in using placebo psychotherapies, and for the definitive study we are considering the use of alternative comparison groups involving a nonintervention control and/or a supportive treatment control administered by an independent therapist who is not also involved with the treatment group. One practical difficulty with involvement of independent therapists or with nonintervention is that of keeping assessors truly "blind." In trials of any management strategy (psychotherapeutic or pharmacological), however much participants are asked to avoid mentioning aspects of therapy, identity of therapists, or side effects experienced, they frequently do so inadvertently. There seems to be no ideal methodology, but this does not excuse us from attempting to use the best available—or, as we are intending, a variety of the best alternatives. Initially, this will involve evaluation of a management package; if this proves successful, we can then progress to evaluation of the individual components utilized.

Discussion and debate are needed also about whether the conclusions drawn from the research cited earlier are warranted. Is the conclusion we have drawn and acted upon—that symptoms of schizophrenia are on functional continua with normality—justified? Are the phenomena observed in organic psychoses and/or deprivation states really related to schizophrenia? Is it reasonable to use similarities between beliefs in supernatural phenomena and certain delusions and thought disorders as a basis for therapeutic intervention? Does the concept of "delusion" need to be radically re-examined, particularly in the light of the evidence about "normal" belief formation? Is it possible, as we contend, to establish and maintain a good rapport with most people with schizophrenia? And with such a rapport, do delusions generally become understandable, with time and patience?

Any process of treatment should evolve in response to circumstances and the process of scientific evaluation. Analytical psychotherapy in this area has perhaps failed to make progress because of the lack of such critical endeavor. Cognitive therapy draws its strength from its scientific rationalism—its hypothesis setting and testing. The hypotheses we present here must be subject to "trial by fire"; we advise you to remain skeptical of them and welcome you to participate in their evaluation and evolution.

Aggernaes, A. (1972). The experienced reality of hallucinations and other psychological phenomena. *Acta Psychiatrica Scandinavica, 48,* 220–238.

Allen, T. E., & Agus, B. (1968). Hyperventilation leading to hallucinations. *American Journal of Psychiatry, 125,* 632–637.

American Psychiatric Association, Task Force on DSM-IV. (1993, March 1). *DSM-IV draft criteria.* Washington, DC: Author.

Andersson, B.-O., Turesson, P., Skagerlind, E., et al. (1989). *Preliminary results of an intensive cognitive-behavioral treatment programme for patients with schizophrenic symptoms.* Paper presented at the World Congress of Cognitive Therapy, Oxford.

Argyle, M. (1978). Non-verbal communication and mental disorder [Editorial]. *Psychological Medicine, 8,* 551–553.

Arieti, S. (1974). *Interpretation of schizophrenia* (2nd ed.). New York: Basic Books.

Arieti, S. (1979). *Understanding and helping the schizophrenic.* Harmondsworth, England: Penguin.

Arthur, A. Z. (1964). Theories and explanations of delusions. *American Journal of Psychiatry, 121,* 105–115.

Asaad, G., & Shapiro, B. (1986). Hallucinations: Theoretical and clinical overview. *American Journal of Psychiatry, 143*(9), 1088–1097.

Ascher-Svanum, H. (1989). A psychoeducational intervention for schizophrenic patients. *Patient Education and Counselling, 14,* 81–87.

Ayer, A. (1964). One's knowledge of others' minds. In D. A. Gustafson, (Ed.), *Essays in philosophical psychology.* London: Macmillan.

Bateson, G., Jackson, D. D., Haley, J., et al. (1956). Toward a theory of schizophrenia. *Behavioral Science, 1,* 251–264.

Bebbington, P. (1990). *Life events and classification of schizophrenia.* Paper presented at the Schizophrenia 1990 Conference, Vancouver, British Columbia.

Bebbington, P., Wilkins, S., Jones, P. B., et al. (1993). Life events and psychosis: Initial results from the Camberwell Collaborative Psychosis Study. *British Journal of Psychiatry, 162,* 72–79.

Beck, A. T. (1952). Successful outpatient psychotherapy of a chronic schizophrenic with a delusion based on borrowed guilt. *Psychiatry, 15,* 305–312.

Beck, A. T., Emery, G., & Greenberg, R. L. (1985). *Anxiety disorders and phobias: A cognitive perspective.* New York: Basic Books.

Beck, A. T., Freeman, A., & Associates. (1990). *Cognitive therapy of personality disorders.* New York: Guilford Press.

Beck, A. T., Rush, A. J., Shaw, B. F., & Emery, G. (1979). *Cognitive therapy of depression.* New York: Guilford Press.

Bentall, R., & Slade, P. D. (1985). Reality testing and auditory hallucinations: A signal detection analysis. *British Journal of Clinical Psychology, 24,* 159–169.

Bexton, W. H., Heron, W., & Scott, T. H. (1954). Effects of decreased variation in the sensory environment. *Canadian Journal of Psychology, 8*(2), 70–76.

Birchwood, M., & Cochrane, R. (1990). Families coping with schizophrenia: Coping styles, their origins and correlates. *Psychological Medicine, 20,* 857–865.

Bleuler, M. (1974). The long-term course of the schizophrenic psychosis. *Psychological Medicine, 4,* 244–254.

Boker, W., Brenner, H. D., & Wurgler, S. (1989). Vulnerability-linked deficiencies, psychopathology and coping behavior of schizophrenics and their relatives. *British Journal of Psychiatry, 155* (Suppl. 5), 128–135.

Breier, A., & Strauss, J. S. (1983). Self-control in psychotic disorders. *Archives of General Psychiatry, 40,* 1141–1145.

Brenner, H. D. (1989). The treatment of basic psychological dysfunctions from a systemic point of view. *British Journal of Psychiatry, 155* (Suppl. 5), 74–83.

Brenner H. D., Boker, W., Muller, J., et al. (1987). On autoprotective efforts of schizophrenics, neurotics and controls. *Acta Psychiatrica Scandinavica, 75,* 405–414.

Brett-Jones, J., Garety, P., & Hemsley, D. (1987). Measuring delusional experiences: A method and its application. *British Journal of Clinical Psychology, 26,* 257–265.

Brooks, G. W., Deane, W. N., & Hugel, R. W. (1968). Some aspects of the subjective experience of schizophrenia. *Diseases of the Nervous System, 29* (Suppl. 5), 78–82.

Brown, G. W., & Birley, J. L. T. (1968). Crises and life changes and the onset of schizophrenia. *Journal of Health and Social Behavior, 9,* 203–214.

Brown, G. W., Birley, J. L. T., & Wing, J. (1972). Influence of family life on the course of schizophrenic disorders: A replication. *British Journal of Psychiatry, 121,* 241–258.

Buchanan, A. (1992). A two-year prospective study of treatment compliance in patients with schizophrenia. *Psychological Medicine, 22,* 787–797.

Carpenter, W. T. (1984). A perspective on the Psychotherapy of Schizophrenia Project. *Schizophrenia Bulletin, 10*(4), 599–602.

Carr, V. (1988). Patients' techniques for coping with schizophrenia: An exploratory study. *British Journal of Medical Psychology, 61,* 339–352.

Chandiramani, K., & Varma, V. K. (1987). Imagery in schizophrenic patients compared with normal controls. *British Journal of Medical Psychology, 60,* 335–341.

Ciompi, L. (1984). Is there really a schizophrenia? The long term course of psychotic phenomena. *British Journal of Psychiatry, 145,* 636–640.

Claridge, G. (1972). The schizophrenias as nervous types. *British Journal of Psychiatry, 121,* 1–17.

Cohen, C. I., & Berk, L. A. (1985). Personal coping styles of schizophrenic outpatients. *Hospital and Community Psychiatry, 36*(4), 407–410.

Collins, M. N., Cull, C. A., & Sireling, L. (1989). Pilot study of persistent auditory hallucinations by modified auditory input. *British Medical Journal, 299,* 431–432.

Cox, D., & Cowling, P. (1989). *Are you normal?* London: Tower Press.

Cramer, P., Weegman, M., & O'Neil, M. (1989). Schizophrenia and the perception of emotions. *British Journal of Psychiatry, 155,* 225–228.

Critchley, E. M. R., & Rossall, C. J. (1978). Hallucinations. *British Journal of Hospital Medicine, 19,* 64–69.

Crowcroft, A. (1967). *The psychotic.* Harmondsworth, England: Penguin.

Cutting, J., & Murphy, D. (1988). Schizophrenic thought disorder. *British Journal of Psychiatry, 152,* 310–319.

David, A. S. (1990). Insight and psychosis. *British Journal of Psychiatry, 156,* 798–808.

Dryden, W. (1985). *Therapist's dilemmas.* London: Harper & Row.

Dulit, E. (1972). Adolescent thinking à la Piaget: The formal stage. *Journal of Youth and Adolescence, 1*(4), 282–301.

Eckman, T., Wirshing, W. C., Marder, S. R., et al. (1992). Technique for training schizophrenic patients in illness self-management: A controlled trial. *American Journal of Psychiatry, 11,* 1549–1555.

Elkin, I., Shea, T., Watkins, J. T., et al. (1989). National Institute of Mental Health Treatment of Depression Collaborative Research Program: General effectiveness of treatments. *Archives of General Psychiatry, 46,* 971–982.

Ellis, A. (1962). *Reason and emotion in psychotherapy.* New York: Lyle Stewart.

Erikson, E. H. (1965). *Childhood and society.* Harmondsworth, England: Penguin.

Eysenck, H. J. (1986). Theories of parapsychological phenomena. *Encyclopedia Britannica, 15,* 1002.

Falloon, I. R. H. (1984). Stress and schizophrenia. In S. R. Hirsch (Ed.), *Schizophrenia.* London: Update.

Falloon, I. R. H., & Talbot, R. E. (1981). Persistent auditory hallucinations: Coping mechanisms and implications for management. *Psychological Medicine, 11,* 329–339.

Farde, L., Wiesel, F., Halldin, C., et al. (1988). Central D-2 dopamine receptor occupancy in schizophrenic patients treated with anti-psychotic drugs. *Archives of General Psychiatry, 45,* 71–76.

Federn, P. (1952). *Ego psychology and the psychoses.* New York: Basic Books.

Ferguson, B. (1990). Clinical Audit. *Psychiatric Bulletin, 14,* 275–277.

Fischman, L. G. (1983). Dreams, hallucinogenic drug states, and schizophrenia: A psychological and biological comparison. *Schizophrenia Bulletin, 9,* 73–94.

Fischoff, B., & Bayeth-Marom, R. (1983). Hypothesis testing from a Bayesian perspective. *Psychological Review, 90,* 239–260.

Fisher, E. B., & Winkler, R. C. (1975). Self-control over intrusive experiences. *Journal of Consulting and Clinical Psychology, 43,* 911–916.

Foudraine, J. (1974). *Not made of wood.* Tiptree, Essex: Anchor.

Fowler, D., & Morley, S. (1989). The cognitive–behavioural treatment of hallucinations and delusions: A preliminary study. *Behavioural Psychotherapy, 17,* 267–282.

Frank, J. D. (1973). *Persuasion and healing.* Baltimore: Johns Hopkins University Press.

Frankl, V. (1959). *Man's search for meaning.* New York: Beacon.

Freeman, T., Cameron, J. L., & McGhie, A. (1958). *Chronic schizophrenia.* New York: International Universities Press.

Freud, S. (1961). *The complete psychological works of Sigmund Freud* (Vol. 12). London: Hogarth.

Fromkin, V., & Rodman, R. (1988). *An introduction to language* (4th ed.). New York: Holt, Rinehart & Winston.

Fromm-Reichmann, F. (1953). *Principles of intensive psychotherapy.* London: Allen & Unwin.

Goffman, E. (1961). *Asylums.* New York: Doubleday/Anchor.

Gottesman, I. I., & Shields, J. (1982). *Schizophrenia: The epigenetic puzzle.* Cambridge, England: Cambridge University Press.

Grassian, G. (1983). Psychopathology of solitary confinement. *American Journal of Psychiatry, 140,* 1450–1454.

Greenwood, V. B. (1984). Cognitive therapy with the young adult chronic patient. In: A. Freeman & V. B. Greenwood (Eds.), *Cognitive therapy: Applications in psychiatric and medical settings.* New York: Human Sciences Press.

Groves, T. (1990). After the asylums: The local picture. *British Medical Journal, 300,* 1128–1130.

Gunderson, J. G., Frank, A. F., Katz, H. M., et al. (1984). Effects of psychotherapy in schizophrenia: II. Comparative outcome of two forms of treatment. *Schizophrenia Bulletin, 10,* 564–598.

Hadas, M. (1962). *Essential works of Stoicism.* New York: Bantam.

Hamilton, M. (1984). *Fish's schizophrenia* (3rd ed.). Bristol, England: Wright.

Harding, C. M., McCormick, R. V., Strauss, J. S., et al. (1989). Computerised life chart methods to map domains of function and illustrate patterns of interactions in the long-term course trajectories of patients who once met the criteria for DSM-III schizophrenia. *British Journal of Psychiatry, 155*(Suppl. 5), 100–106.

Harrow, M., & Prosen, M. (1978). Intermingling and disordered logic as influences on schizophrenic "thought disorders." *Archives of General Psychiatry, 35,* 1213–1218.

Hartman, L. M., & Cashman, F. E. (1983) Cognitive–behavioural and psychopharmacological treatment of delusional symptoms: A preliminary report. *Behavioural Psychotherapy, 11,* 50–61.

Hatfield, A. B. (1989). Patients' accounts of stress and coping in schizophrenia. *Hospital and Community Psychiatry, 40,* 1141–1145.

Hemsley, D. R. (1986). Schizophrenia: Treatment. In S. Lindsay & G. Powell, (Eds.), *A handbook of clinical psychology.* London: Gower.

Hemsley, D. R., & Garety, P. A. (1986). The formation and maintenance of delusions: A Bayesian analysis. *British Journal of Psychiatry, 149,* 51–56.

Hirsch, S. R., & Jolley, A. G. (1989). The dysphoric syndrome in schizophrenia and its implications for relapse. *British Journal of Psychiatry, 155* (Suppl. 5), 46–50.

Hogarty, G. E., Goldberg, S. C., & The Collaborative Study Group. (1973). Drugs and sociotherapy in the aftercare of schizophrenic patients: One year relapse rates. *Archives of General Psychiatry, 28,* 54–64.

Hole, R. W., Rush, A. J., & Beck, A. T. (1979). A cognitive investigation of schizophrenic delusions. *Psychiatry, 42,* 312–319.

Hudson, L. (1975). *Human beings: An introduction to the psychology of human experience.* Bungay, England: Triad Paladin.

Jacobs, L. I. (1980). A cognitive approach to persistent delusions. *American Journal of Psychotherapy, 34,* 556–563.

Jaspers, K. (1963). *General psychopathology* (J. Hoenig & M. W. Hamilton, Trans.). Manchester, England: Manchester University Press. (Original work published 1913)

Jaynes, J. (1976). *The origin of consciousness in the bicameral mind.* Boston: Houghton Mifflin.

Johnstone, E. C., Owens, D. G. C., Gold, A., et al. (1984). Schizophrenic patients discharged from hospital—a follow-up study. *British Journal of Psychiatry, 145,* 586–590.

Joyce, J. (1969). *Ulysses*. Harmondsworth, England: Penguin. (Original work published 1922)

Judkins, M., & Slade, P. (1981). A questionnaire study of hostility in persistent auditory hallucinators. *British Journal of Medical Psychology, 54,* 243–250.

Kaney, S., & Bentall, R. P. (1989). Persecutory delusions and attributional style. *British Journal of Medical Psychology, 62,* 191–198.

Kay, D. W. K., & Roth, M. (1961). Environmental and hereditary factors in the schizophrenia of old age ('late paraphrenia') and their bearing in the general problem of causation in schizophrenia. *Journal of Mental Science, 107,* 649–686.

Kind, H. (1966). The psychogenesis of schizophrenia. *British Journal of Psychiatry, 112,* 333–349.

Kingdon, D. G., & Bakewell, E. (1988). Aggressive behaviour: Evaluation of a non-seclusion policy of a district psychiatric service. *British Journal of Psychiatry, 153,* 631–634.

Kingdon, D. G., & Turkington, D. (1991a). Preliminary report: The use of cognitive behavior therapy and a normalizing rationale in schizophrenia. *Journal of Nervous and Mental Disease, 179,* 207–211.

Kingdon, D. G., & Turkington, D. (1991b). A role for cognitive therapy in schizophrenia? [Editorial]. *Social Psychiatry & Psychiatric Epidemiology, 26,* 101–103.

Kingdon, D. G., Turkington, D., Collis, J., et al. (1989) Befriending: Cost-effective community care. *Psychiatric Bulletin, 13,* 350–351.

Kingdon, D. G., Turkington, D., Malcolm, K., et al. (1991) Replacing the mental hospital: Community provision for a district's chronically psychiatrically disabled in domestic environments. *British Journal of Psychiatry, 158,* 113–116.

Kraupl-Taylor, F. (1981). On pseudo-hallucinations. *Psychological Medicine, 11,* 265–271.

Kissling, W. (1992). Ideal and reality of neuroleptic relapse prevention. *British Journal of Psychiatry, 161,* (Suppl. 18), 133–139.

Kuipers, L., & Bebbington, P. (1987). *Living with mental illness: A book for relatives and friends.* London: Souvenir.

Laing, R. D. (1960). *The divided self.* Harmondsworth, England: Penguin.

Laing, R. D., & Esterson, A. (1964). *Sanity, madness and the family.* Harmondsworth, England: Penguin.

Leff, J. P. (1968). Perceptual phenomena and personality in sensory deprivation. *British Journal of Psychiatry, 114,* 1499–1508.

Leff, J. P., Berkowitz, R., Eberlein-Fries, R., & Kuipers, L. (1987). *Notes for relatives and friends.* London: National Schizophrenia Fellowship.

Leff, J. P., & Vaughn, C. (1980). The interaction of life events and relatives' expressed emotion in schizophrenia and depressive neurosis. *British Journal of Psychiatry, 136,* 146–153.

Levy, S. T., McGlashan, T. H., & Carpenter, W. T. (1975). Integration and sealing-over as recovery styles from acute psychosis. *Journal of Nervous and Mental Disease, 161,* 307–312.

Lindqvist, P., & Allebeck, P. (1990). Schizophrenia and crime. *British Journal of Psychiatry, 157,* 345–350.

Lowe, C. F., & Chadwick, P. D. J. (1990). Verbal control of delusions. *Behavior Therapy, 21,* 461–479.

Ludwig, A. M. (1966). Altered states of consciousness. *Archives of General Psychiatry, 15,* 225–234.

Lukoff, D., Snyder, K., Ventura, J., et al. (1984). Life events, familial stress, and coping in the developmental course of schizophrenia. *Schizophrenia Bulletin, 10,* 258–292.

MacCarthy, B., Benson, J., & Brewin, C. R. (1986). Task motivation and problem appraisal in long-term psychiatric patients. *Psychological Medicine, 16,* 431–438.

MacMillan, J. F., Crow, T. J., Johnson, A. L., et al. (1986). The Northwick Park Study of first episodes of schizophrenia. III. Short-term outcome in trial entrants and trial eligible patients. *British Journal of Psychiatry, 148,* 128–133.

Mayou, R. (1984). Sick role, illness behaviour and coping. *British Journal of Psychiatry, 144,* 320–322.

McKenna, P. J. (1984). Overvalued ideas. *British Journal of Psychiatry, 145,* 579–585.

Meichenbaum, D., & Cameron, R. (1973). Training schizophrenics to talk to themselves: A means of developing attentional controls. *Behavior Therapy, 4,* 515–534.

Meltzer, H. Y., Kupfer, D. J., Wyatt, R., et al. (1970). Sleep disturbance and serum CPK activity in acute psychosis. *Archives of General Psychiatry, 22,* 398–405.

Miller, L. J., O'Connor, E., & DePasquale, T. (1993). Patients' attitudes to hallucinations. *American Journal of Psychiatry, 150,* 584–588.

Milton, F., Patwa, V. K., & Hafner, R. J. (1978). Confrontation vs. belief modification in persistently deluded patients. *British Journal of Medical Psychology, 51,* 127–130.

Murray, R. M. (1984). Prognostic factors in schizophrenia. In S. R. Hirsch (Ed.), *Schizophrenia.* London: Update.

Murray, R. M., Kerwin, R. W., & Nimgaonkar, V. (1988). What have we learned about the biology of schizophrenia? In K. Granville-Grossman (Ed.), *Recent advances in psychiatry* (Vol. 6). London: Churchill Livingstone.

Nelson, H. E., Thrasher, S., & Barnes, T. R. E. (1991). Practical ways of alleviating auditory hallucinations. *British Medical Journal, 302,* 327.

Neuchterlein, K. L., Goldstein, M. J., Ventura, J., et al. (1989). Patient environment relationships in schizophrenia: Information processing, communication deviance, autonomic arousal, and stressful life events. *British Journal of Psychiatry, 155*(Suppl. 5), 84–89.

Oswald, I. (1974). *Sleep* (3rd ed.). Harmondsworth, England: Penguin.

Parloff, M. B. (1986). Placebo controls in psychotherapy research: A sine qua non or a placebo for research problems? *Journal of Consulting and Clinical Psychology, 54*, 79–87.

Parnas, J., Schulsinger, F., Mednick, S. A., et al. (1982) Behavioral precursors of schizophrenia spectrum. *Archives of General Psychiatry, 39*, 658–664.

Perris, C. (1988). *Cognitive therapy with schizophrenic patients.* New York: Cassell.

Piaget, J. (1973). *The child's conception of the world* (J. A. Tomlinson, Trans.). St. Albans, England: Paladin. (Original work published 1929)

Pym, B. (1989, April 6). Run it your own way. *Community Care*, 17–19.

Rachman, S. (1983). Irrational thinking, with special reference to cognitive therapy. *Advances in Behavioral Therapy, 5*, 63–68.

Rakfeldt, J., & Strauss, J. S. (1989). The low turning point: A control mechanism in the course of mental disorder. *Journal of Nervous and Mental Disease, 177*, 32–37.

Reed, J. (1970). Schizophrenic thought disorder: A review and hypothesis. *Comprehensive Psychiatry, 11*, 1–30.

Roberts, G. (1992). The origins of delusion. *British Journal of Psychiatry, 161*, 298–308.

Romme, M. A. J., & Escher, A. D. M. A. C. (1989). Hearing voices. *Schizophrenia Bulletin, 15*, 209–216.

Romme, M. A. J., Honig, A., Noorthoorn, E. O., & Escher, A. D. M. A. C. (1992). Coping with hearing voices: An emancipatory approach. *British Journal of Psychiatry, 161*, 99–103.

Rosen, J. N. (1953). *Direct analysis.* New York: Grune & Stratton.

Rudden, M., Gilmore, M., & Frances, A. (1982). Delusions: When to confront the facts of life. *American Journal of Psychiatry, 139*, 929–932.

Rutter, D. R. (1985). Language in schizophrenia. *British Journal of Psychiatry, 146*, 399–404.

Sacks, M. H., Carpenter, W. T., & Strauss, J. S. (1974). Recovery from delusions. *Archives of General Psychiatry, 30*, 117–120.

Satel, S. L., & Sledge, W. H. (1989). Audiotape playback as a technique in treatment of schizophrenic patients. *American Journal of Psychiatry, 146*, 1012–1016.

Scharfetter, C. (1980). *General psychopathology* (H. Marshall, Trans.). Cambridge, England: Cambridge University Press.

Scheff, T. J. (1963). The role of the mentally ill and the dynamics of mental disorder: A research framework. *Sociometry, 26*, 436–453.

Schneider, K. (1973). The concept of delusion. In S. R. Hirsch & M. Shepherd

(Eds.), *Themes and variations in European psychiatry: An anthology.* Bristol, England: Wright.

Sedman, G. (1966a). A comparative study of pseudohallucinations, imagery and true hallucinations. *British Journal of Psychiatry, 112,* 9–17.

Sedman, G. (1966b). 'Inner voices.' *British Journal of Psychiatry, 112,* 485–490.

Siegel, R. K. (1984). Hostage hallucinations. *Journal of Nervous and Mental Disease, 172,* 264–271.

Slade, P. D. (1973). The psychological investigation and treatment of auditory hallucinations: A second case report. *British Journal of Medical Psychology, 46,* 293–296.

Slade, P. D. (1976). Hallucinations [Editorial]. *Psychological Medicine, 6,* 7–13.

Slade, P. D. (1984). Sensory deprivation and clinical psychiatry. *British Journal of Hospital Medicine, 32,* 256–260.

Slade, P. D., & Bentall, R. (1989). Psychological treatment for negative symptoms. *British Journal of Psychiatry, 155*(Suppl. 7), 133–135.

Smyth, P. (1990). *Delusional symptoms related to TV viewing.* Paper presented at the Fourth Leeds Psychopathology Symposium, Leeds, England.

Spitzer, R. L., Endicott, J., & Robins, R. (1975). *Research Diagnostic Criteria (RDC) for a selected group of functional disorders.* New York: Department of Biometrics, New York State Psychiatric Institute.

Stanton, A. H., Gunderson, J. G., Knapp, P. H., et al. (1984). Effects of psychotherapy in schizophrenia: I. Design and implementation of a controlled study. *Schizophrenia Bulletin, 10,* 520–562.

Stevenson, I. (1983). Do we need a new word to supplement "hallucination?" *American Journal of Psychiatry, 140,* 1609–1611.

Strauss, J. S. (1969). Hallucinations and delusions as points on continua function. *Archives of General Psychiatry, 21,* 581–586.

Strauss, J. S. (1989). Mediating processes in schizophrenia. *British Journal of Psychiatry, 155*(Suppl 5), 22–28.

Strauss, J. S., Rakfeldt, J., Harding, C. M., & Lieberman, P. (1989). Psychological and social aspects of negative symptoms. *British Journal of Psychiatry, 155*(Suppl 7), 128–132.

Sturgeon, D., Kuipers, L., Berkowitz, R., et al. (1981). Psychophysiological responses of schizophrenic patients to high and low expressed emotion relatives. *British Journal of Psychiatry, 138,* 40–45.

Sullivan, H. S. (1962). *Schizophrenia as a human process.* New York: Norton.

Tarrier, N. (1987). An investigation of residual psychotic symptoms in discharged schizophrenic patients. *British Journal of Clinical Psychology, 26,* 141–143.

Tarrier, N., Beckett, R., Harwood, S., et al. (1993). A trial of two cognitive-behavioural methods of treating drug-resistant residual psychotic symptoms in schizophrenic patients: I. Outcome. *British Journal of Psychiatry, 162,* 524–532.

Tarrier, N., Harwood, S., Yussof, L., et al. (1990). Coping strategy enhancement (C. S. E.): A method of treating residual schizophrenic symptoms. *Behavioural Psychotherapy 18*, 643–662.

Tarrier, N., Vaughn, C., Lader, M. H., et al. (1979). Bodily reactions to people and events in schizophrenia. *Archives of General Psychiatry, 36*, 311–315.

Taylor, P. J., & Gunn, J. (1984). Violence and psychosis. I. Risk of violence amongst psychotic men. *British Medical Journal, 288*, 1945–1949.

Tien, A. Y. (1992). Distribution of hallucinations in the population. *Social Psychiatry and Psychiatric Epidemiology, 26*, 287–292.

Tissot, R., & Bernand, Y. (1980). Aspects of cognitive activity in schizophrenia. *Psychological Medicine, 10*, 657–663.

Tolstoy, N. (1985). *The quest for Merlin*. Sevenoaks, England: Sceptre.

Trower, P., Bryant, B., & Argyle, M. (1978). *Social skills and mental health*. London: Methuen.

Truax, C. B., & Carkhuff, R. R. (1967). *Toward effective counselling and psychotherapy*. Chicago: Aldine.

Turkington, D., & Kingdon, D. G. (1991). Ordering thoughts in thought disorder. *British Journal of Psychiatry, 159*, 160–161.

Turkington, D., Kingdon, D. G., & Malcolm, K. (1991). The use of an unstaffed flat for crisis intervention and rehabilitation. *Psychiatric Bulletin, 15*, 13–14.

Turkington, D., Larkin, E., & Kingdon, D. G. (1990). Patient and relative attitudes to mental hospital closure and transfer to a hospital hostel. *Psychiatric Bulletin, 14*, 717–718.

Tyrer, P., Sievewright, N., Kingdon, D., et al. (1988). The Nottingham study of neurotic disorder: Comparison of drug and psychological treatments. *Lancet, ii*, 235–240.

Tyrer, P., Sievewright, N., Murphy, S., et al. (1990). The Nottingham study of neurotic disorder: Relationship between personality status and symptoms. *Psychological Medicine, 20*, 423–431.

Van Putten, T., Crumpton, E., & Yale, C. (1976). Drug refusal and the wish to be crazy. *Archives of General Psychiatry, 33*, 1443–1446.

Vernon, J. (1963). *Inside the black room*. Harmondsworth, England: Penguin.

Walker, E., McGuire, M., & Bettes, B. (1984) Recognition and identification of facial stimuli by schizophrenics and patients with affective disorders. *British Journal of Clinical Psychology, 23*, 37–44.

Watt, D. C., Katz, K., & Shepherd, M. (1983). The natural history of schizophrenia: A five year prospective follow-up of a representative sample of schizophrenics by means of a standardized clinical and social assessment. *Psychological Medicine, 13*, 663–670.

Watts, F. N., Powell, G. E., & Austin, S. V. (1983). Modification of delusional beliefs. *British Journal of Medical Psychology, 46*, 359–363.

Wilcox, J., Briones, D., & Suess, L. (1991). Auditory hallucinations, posttraumatic stress disorder and ethnicity. *Comprehensive Psychiatry*, 320–323.

Williams, E. (1974). An analysis of gaze in schizophrenics. *British Journal of Social and Clinical Psychology, 13*, 1–8.

Wing, J. K. (1987). Psychosocial factors affecting the long-term course of schizophrenia. In J. S. Strauss, W. Boker, & H. D. Brenner (Eds.), *Psychosocial treatment of schizophrenia*. Toronto: Huber.

Wing, J. K., Cooper, J. E., & Sartorius, N. (1974). *The measurement and classification of psychiatric symptoms*. Cambridge, England: Cambridge University Press.

World Health Organization. (1973). *International Pilot Study of Schizophrenia*. (Vol. 1). Geneva: Author.

World Health Organization. (1989). *International classification of diseases* (10th rev., draft). Geneva: Author.

World Health Organization. (1992). *The ICD-10 classification of mental and behavioral disorders: Clinical descriptions and diagnostic guidelines*. Geneva: Author.

Wright, D. S., Taylor, A., Roy Davies, D., et al. (1970). *Introducing psychology: An experimental approach*. Harmondsworth, England: Penguin.

Wykes, T. (1980). Language and schizophrenia [Editorial]. *Psychological Medicine, 10*, 403–406.

Zubin, J., & Spring, B. (1977). Vulnerability—a new view on schizophrenia. *Journal of Abnormal Psychology, 86*, 103–126.

Zubin, J., & Steinhauer, S. (1981). How to break the logjam in schizophrenia. *Journal of Nervous and Mental Disease, 169*, 477–492.